Public Relations in Asia Pacific

Communicating Effectively Across Cultures

Public Relations in Asia Pacific
Communicating Effectively Across Cultures

MARY M. DEVEREUX

ANNE PEIRSON-SMITH

WILEY

John Wiley & Sons (Asia) Pte. Ltd.

Copyright © 2009 John Wiley & Sons (Asia) Pte. Ltd.
Published in 2009 by John Wiley & Sons (Asia) Pte. Ltd.
2 Clementi Loop, #02-01, Singapore 129809

This publication is designed to provide accurate and authoritative information in regard to the subject matter covered. It is sold with the understanding that the publisher is not engaged in rendering professional services. If professional advice or other expert assistance is required, the services of a competent professional person should be sought.

Neither the authors nor the publisher are liable for any actions prompted or caused by the information presented in this book. Any views expressed herein are those of the authors and do not represent the views of the organizations they work for.

Other Wiley Editorial Offices

John Wiley & Sons, 111 River Street, Hoboken, NJ 07030, USA

John Wiley & Sons, The Atrium, Southern Gate, Chichester, West Sussex, P019 8SQ, United Kingdom

John Wiley & Sons (Canada) Ltd., 5353 Dundas Street West, Suite 400, Toronto, Ontario, M9B 6HB, Canada

John Wiley & Sons Australia Ltd, 42 McDougall Street, Milton, Queensland 4064, Australia

Wiley-VCH, Boschstrasse 12, D-69469 Weinheim, Germany

Library of Congress Cataloging-in-Publication Data

ISBN 978-0-470-82430-6

Typeset in 11.5/14.5pt Sabon-Roman by Thomson Digital.

Printed in Singapore by Saik Wah Press Pte. Ltd.

10 9 8 7 6 5 4 3 2 1

Contents

Preface

As the saying goes: "If you want to prepare a fresh omelet for breakfast, go out and buy a hen." We could not find a book focusing on the realities of public relations in Asia Pacific, so we decided to write one.

As practitioners and educators in public relations for over 20 years, most of these located in the Asia Pacific region (including Hong Kong, China, Korea, and Australia), we recognized the need to collate our experience and provide an insider's viewpoint on this dynamic industry. To that end, we intend this book to be useful for several audiences: for students of the subject, as they prepare for a career in public relations; for practitioners in the region, who will find this a useful resource to assist in professional development; and for executives who just want to learn more about the industry, given its growing importance in corporate practice.

This book provides key insights into the rapid expansion of public relations in the Asia Pacific region, based on the required theory and practice needed to communicate effectively with stakeholders across different cultures and geographies. In the past two decades, public relations has taken on a new importance. As the world has globalized, so have domestic Asia Pacific organizations, in both the public and private sector, entered wider markets or received foreign investment. This requires them to deal with a wide variety of audiences, including consumers, investors, government officials, pressure groups, competitors, and the media.

More than ever, the recent global economic downturn has highlighted the need to communicate positive organizational messages to these audiences and to their influencers, in order to gain acknowledgment for their achievements and to ensure competitive survival.

Each chapter of this book covers the essential concepts and skills of public relations across the core practices of the profession. These include public and government affairs, marketing communications, branding, media relations, healthcare, corporate and financial communications, issues and crisis management, internal and change management, and corporate social responsibility. The application and impact of digital media is also used as a common unifying theme throughout, to mirror topical developments in the public relations profession.

Case studies and examples from Australia, China, Hong Kong, India, Indonesia, Japan, Korea, Malaysia, Philippines, New Zealand, Singapore, Taiwan, Thailand, and Vietnam can be found in each chapter, bringing the strategic and tactical practices of public relations into sharp focus. In addition, we have sought the expert insights of experienced communication professionals working around the region.

We would like to thank the many public relations professionals who have contributed to the collective knowledge upon which this book is based. In addition, we thank everyone at John Wiley & Sons (Asia), in particular Nick Wallwork and Fiona Wong, who helped breathe life into this project, and Joel Balbin and his efficient editing team, who shepherded the book into publication.

CHAPTER 1

Public Relations in Asia Pacific

- An IT company is rebranding, following a takeover deal, and launching its new corporate logo in Singapore
- A new CEO of a multinational oil company based in Malaysia is giving an inaugural speech to the local chamber of commerce, including senior government officials
- A soft drinks manufacturer is relaunching an existing product with a new flavor for the Taiwanese market
- A charity for abandoned children in India is trying to raise funds to build a series of new children's homes across several cities
- A government department in Jakarta is responsible for health plans to educate young people about the dangers of taking drugs
- A power company in Japan plans to fund a series of wind farms as an alternative to traditional sources of energy
- A magnate in Macau donates billions of dollars to build a new private university
- A soy sauce manufacturer based in China is recalling its product from all supermarket shelves across Asia as government food and safety departments have found toxic deposits in bottles produced at its plant in Tianjin
- Compromising images of a music celebrity from Australia start to circulate the Internet while the tabloid media publish an exclusive story with a modified version of one of the photographs
- An anti-race demonstration in New Zealand gets out of hand with injuries both to protestors and police receiving global media coverage
- Architects in Hong Kong are lobbying the relevant government departments and developers to protect more green urban spaces in the center of the city

What should all of the key participants in these scenarios do? If they are to prosper in their respective industry sectors, they may choose a suitable public relations remedy. This could be anything: a launch event, a news release, a website, a repositioning campaign, a crisis plan, a corporate rebranding exercise, sponsorship of a community event, a competition, an open house event, a staff newsletter, a corporate video, a bylined article, or a meeting with government officials.

Most books on public relations (PR) as a professional practice kick off with a definition of the business itself, as a way of determining its scope and making the intangible appear tangible or the unknown knowable. Yet, defining PR is a bit like describing an elephant, as it comprises such a unique combination of characteristics that it, in fact, defies description. This usually leaves the readers scratching their heads in an attempt to visualize what PR is and how it works, yet marveling over such an elusive profession that appears to do everything for everyone under the banner of communication. Can it really do so much, for so many, with such a great reward in store for all of those who engage in its magical powers of influence?

You Can't Just "Spin" an Issue or Do a "PR Exercise"

For an industry whose mainstay is the management of communication, there are many common misperceptions about the practice of public relations. Too often, we hear a company's action or initiative described as "a PR exercise" or a company employing a "spin doctor" to perfect its corporate image. The term "spin" and the like are the bane of the PR profession and have been overused to the point of becoming quite meaningless. They are often used derogatively to imply that a company is maybe taking action which is either deceptive or even manipulative.

These terms are bandied about in the media, and are used regularly to describe the negative actions of organizations using whitewashing techniques to cover up the corporate scandals that PR companies are allegedly perpetrating on behalf of their clients, or to expose the techniques of "spin" employed by management teams in organizations failing to successfully communicate with their stakeholders.

So, let's put this misconception to rest forever.

A Chinese Fable

Chan Yu's wife had to go to the market in a hurry. Her son followed on her heels, crying.

"Listen to me," she coaxed her son. "Go on home now. When I return, I will prepare a pig for dinner." So the child stopped crying and returned to the house.

When his wife returned home, Chan Yu went to the pigsty to pick a pig for dinner. His wife hurried after him, saying, "Don't take my words seriously. I was just trying to persuade our son to do what I wanted."

Chan Yu quickly drew his wife aside. "We must keep our word, even to children," he said to his wife. "Children are like a blank sheet of paper. They learn everything from their parents and imitate what they see and hear from these role models. If you lie to your son now, he will learn that lying is acceptable. Once you lie to him and he finds out that you lied, he will never trust you again. This is not the right way to educate children."

And so he killed a pig for dinner.

Moral: Lying to anyone results in loss of trust and damaged long-term relationships.

Labeling a Profession

The only PR association with "spin," as such, is metaphorical. Doing PR is not unlike the circus act of plate spinning. By this, we mean that PR professionals are usually busy working on a number of communication-based activities underpinning a range of PR campaigns. These tasks have to keep their momentum and keep spinning as the campaigns progress, and at no point must they be allowed to fall on the ground only to shatter into broken promises. So, PR is a multi-leveled, multi-tasked communication profession entrusted with the continuous plate spinning activity of ensuring that the organization informs its stakeholders about its activities and their wider impact and significance.

While interviewing a senior public relations consultant recently, in the answer to the question, "How do you explain your job to those outside of the public relations field, including prospective clients?" she replied, "Public relations professionals dread that question. Generally, we're all too busy doing it to explain what it is that we are doing."

Public relations professionals also find specific explanations of what they do to be a challenge, as seen in the wide range of terms referring to public

Case Study

Hosting a fashion show using the longest catwalk in the world on the Great Wall of China, Beijing was a creative way of positioning Fendi (LVMH) as a luxury fashion brand leader and innovator both in China and on the global stage by generating wide media coverage.

The media outreach strategy, which was planned by Fleishmann Hillard, created the pre-event media buzz, set-up exclusive coverage by key media, and managed image distribution post-event.

To realize the integrated brand experience, 400 international guests were also invited to Beijing for a five-day visit around the catwalk event as a key part of the promotional strategy. The campaign was a year in the making, involving overall project planning and implementation, in addition to handling media management, hospitality arrangements, and transport logistics. Licenses and regulatory approvals had to be sanctioned from government and related agencies, while third parties were commissioned for sourcing and production aspects. Sponsorship was provided by the Swire Group, BMW, and the Grand Hyatt.

Fendi is the only luxury goods brand to date to have made its mark by launching a fashion show using the Great Wall as a fashion runway.

Source: Asia Pacific PR Awards 2008.

relations found in job advertisements and company brochures from communications planning to perception and ideas management. This trend is seen in a recent job advertisement for a globally–recognized public relations firm:

> Our activities help organizations build intellectual capital. We help differentiate brands, improve customer loyalty, and motivate employees. We help win the support of key stakeholders by developing informed opinion about products, issues and corporate activities. And to safeguard those assets, no one's better at helping you prepare for, and resolve a crisis.

Public relations has been compared to "perception management"

The term "perception management" has been popular in the last two decades. But can you really expect to "manage perceptions" through public relations? It misses the essential point—that public relations can generate understanding and potentially sway opinion and behavior, but cannot ever "manage" how people see and perceive reality either now or at some point in the future, as this is individually determined.

The simple fact is that no amount of communication will change a problem or an issue—you cannot "spin" a problem. The only way to do this is to take correct and ethical action and demonstrate this in full view. What public relations can do, however, is tell people about an organization's positive actions and achievements. Advertising agency, McCann Erickson, said it well 80 years ago, when it coined its slogan, "Truth Well Told." So, public relations, in reality, is all about an organization doing good things and getting the credit for it—when credit is due, of course. You cannot just talk the talk: it is not enough to say that you are an environmentally sustainable company—you have to demonstrate this with real proof and communicate this in real terms to your audience consistently and repeatedly using a range of communication channels.

Point of View

"We live in an age of discontinuities. Unprecedented political, economic and technological forces are creating a new world order and Asia Pacific—home to over half of the world's population and most of its economic growth—is pivotal. This calls for greater cross-cultural understanding and global governance overarching an enlightened interdependent trade system.

The importance of public relations for Asia in this new multi-polar world cannot be understated. New forces are bypassing traditional intermediaries and conducting authentic unfiltered dialogue between people in companies, across countries and cultures, and amongst constituencies and communities of interests. This demands the continuous reinvention of public relations. PR must adapt to remain relevant in a conversational and interactive future."

Bill Rylance, former Chairman, Asia Pacific and Vice Chairman, Global Development, Burson-Marsteller

---

Exploding the Myths of Public Relations

It is perhaps more efficient to begin with what public relations is not. PR has been much misrepresented as sinister propaganda, blurred with advertising, and has even been equated with escort services employed for the purposes of entertaining clients. Below we present and explode some of the commonly held myths about public relations.

PR = Propaganda

To label public relations as propaganda in the *original* sense of the word is, in fact, quite accurate as it referred to the neutral promotion of a belief system or doctrine. The Western view of propaganda is, of course, a negative one. The same word in China, however, means almost the opposite and is viewed as simply another term for publicity or public relations.

Historically, the word became tainted with negative meaning as a way of labeling the sinister political agendas of 20th century wartime governments and the hidden commercial agendas of capitalist governments. The Oxford Dictionary defines propaganda as, "information that is often biased or misleading used to promote a political cause or point of view."

So, propaganda in this sense came to refer to a one-way communication, conveyed from the organization to the public. And its use in the earlier part of the 20th century and by some of today's non-democratic governments is clearly different from an ideal 21st century view of public relations.

We would contend that in politics and business, the practice of public relations is that of justifying (through communications; most powerfully media relations) practices and policies among all the constituencies affected by such. Far from being seen as an illegitimate feature of professional practice it is widely considered that politicians and businessmen who lack public relations skills are unfit for office. Though, often, we can have a closed mind to PR—if the message being promoted is something of which we approve, we call it public relations. If we disapprove of the message, then we call it propaganda.

However, unlike the propagandist, what companies say about themselves should match our experience of what they do. Using public relations activities as a tool of engagement, an organization tries to gain our attention as a way of enhancing our understanding of an issue so that we might respond more favorably to it. *Dialogue* is the buzzword of the early 21st century. So, while propaganda is simply one-way communication, public relations is focused on two-way or multi-level dialogue. These days, PR welcomes and anticipates the possibility of a company being influenced and its actions altered in the course of on-going feedback from its publics.

PR = Publicity

Publicity is solely focused on gaining editorial coverage across a range of media channels—be it on TV, radio, in newspapers, or via blog sites—and by eliciting an instant reaction from activity in a public venue. Publicity is just one element of the public relations role and it is also a recognized component activity of the marketing mix. Clearly, PR now offers a much wider range of communication techniques in the bid to gain positive recognition on behalf of an organization.

PR = Same as advertising

While advertising and public relations are integral parts of the 360 degree marketing mix from the promotional perspective, they are separate disciplines; the key difference being the audience—advertising goes direct, while PR uses third parties, and, of course, advertising space is paid for by the organization, while PR coverage in the form of newspaper stories and interviews, for example, is not. This means that advertising is a controlled form of communication, as the sponsor pays for the space in which the advertising message is placed, and has control over the content of the message and the location and timing of the message release. In PR terms, the message is potentially uncontrolled in the sense that once the media release is sent out or the media interview is given, we cannot guarantee the outcome of the storyline or the story content. Yet, by using public relations approaches, an organization has an opportunity to influence how others view its activities for the better.

PR = Just one long lunch

If only. This is, of course, an old-fashioned view and not one likely to be shared by today's generation. Sure, when PR was synonymous with publicity, wining and dining the media or the client played an important part of the job. Most practitioners would now regard lunch as an unnecessary intrusion into the working day unless it is a focused working session over a glass or two of water.

PR = The mouthpiece of corporate power

This critique suggests that PR fosters unequal power relations in society as it helps the powerful and wealthy impose their views on a naïve population, manipulating their mindsets. But public relations exists to foster mutually beneficial relationships between an organization and its stakeholders in the public interest. Of course, most organizations exist to make a profit, but that does not mean that the competitive edge is won at the expense of ethical practices as public support is critical for the survival of all corporate entities, as many companies, including Enron and Andersen Consulting, have found to their cost.

Case Study

Since 2003, Australia has been plagued by the worse drought conditions since records began, forcing Australians to reconsider their water management strategies. In response to this critical environmental situation, BlueScope Steel devised a Corporate and Social Responsibility (CSR) campaign to help the community manage water resources more effectively, whilst positioning the organization as a conservation and water harvesting leader.

The purpose of the *Tank A Day Challenge* was to encourage community groups and stakeholders across Australia to assist in remedying the inherent water shortage crisis.

Targeting young stakeholders through primary schools' water conservation initiatives nationwide, BlueScope's campaign donated 200 rainwater tanks each with a 27,000 liter capacity—amounting to one tank for each school every day of the year.

The educational nature of the program was integrated through the primary school curriculum, whilst wider media outreach campaigns disseminated the message to local communities in which the schools were situated to reinforce the initiative.

Schools were asked to enter the competition by making an online registration at the campaign website and articulate why water was a valuable resource for their school. Also, after registration, students were required to answer questions about the water cycle and water conservation in an online

(Continued)

quiz. Winning places were awarded to schools based on the school princi-pal's online submission and the number of students in the school who had filled in the quiz successfully.

The principal of the winning school as third party spokesperson was used at the campaign launch, emphasizing the positive outcomes of hav-ing rainwater tanks installed in primary schools and inspiring other schools to engage with the *Tank A Day* initiative.

As a way of adding credibility and audience reach for the campaign, a one-year media partnership was brokered with national breakfast TV pro-gram, *The Today Show,* whose hosts became ambassadors for the *Tank A Day* campaign covering weekly BlueScope branded announcements of winning schools that were supported by slots featuring these schools.

In anticipation of stakeholders questioning BlueScope's involvement in, and motivations for the program, meetings with Government ministers were scheduled and a grassroots local and regional media campaign initi-ated in the areas that successful primary schools were located.

Follow-up post campaign evaluative research indicated that over 25 percent of the population were aware of the Tank A Day Challenge and linked it to BlueScope's brand name. In addition, many schools across the country purchased water tanks from BlueScope and integrated water ob-servation into awareness the school curriculum. As a follow up BlueScope are planning to extend the initiative across another year into 2009-10 with the promise of another 200 donations of water tanks to primary schools across Australia.

The *Tank A Day Challenge* was lauded by the Asia Pacific PR Awards judging panel for devising an original and relevant link between their organization and Australia's water shortage crisis and establishing itself as a leader in this regard.

The campaign was also considered to demonstrate an effective and sustainable approach to water conservation for the country as it created a new generation of environmental ambassadors in the form of school children—which promises a lasting environmental solution for Bluescope and Australia.

Source: Asia Pacific PR Awards 2008.

PR as a One-Stop Communication Shop

Over the past decade, PR has been seen as one of the most increasingly significant components of the promotional marketing mix, distinguishing itself as good value, sustainable communication, in contrast to potentially expensive and one-way communication advertising.

The strategic integrated communication role assumed by PR beyond the more traditional media management role is now established as having a wider brief to fulfill. The wider value of PR is now to be found in alerting, creating, and managing trends, and influencing and impacting public opinion through finely tuned messages directed at a universe of stakeholders who are encouraged to engage in critical dialogue.

So, although a significant amount of time is devoted to tactical communications, increasingly, public relations managers operate at more strategic levels, directing research into stakeholder perceptions and counseling management about the implementation of communication campaigns or prompting them to prepare for crises or audit their ethical practices, which clearly represents a move away from old perceptions of a predominantly publicity-oriented profession. Not only has PR raised its head above the line and is no longer content to be the sidekick of above-the-line advertising, it has actually dispensed with the line altogether.

We can go further to suggest that within an organization and in its external relationships with stakeholders, every element of communication has a PR aspect. The competitive survival of all organizations now depends on communicating with stakeholders—getting the right messages across to the right audience at the right time in the most appropriate and meaningful way.

PR on the job: What do PR professionals do?

Two of the main roles for the public relations professional focus on the communication technician and the communication manager. The former highly-skilled role involves communications programs and activities such as writing media releases, editing newsletters, developing websites and generally is not involved in organizational decision-making. The second role of the public relations professional positions him as an integral part of the senior team which plans, manages, and facilitates the communications program, counsels management, and makes policy decisions as an intermediary between senior management and the workforce, organization and competitor, and organization and customer. In this sense, most public relations professionals play both manager and technician roles as part of their job.

How to tell the PR story

We are all inveterate storytellers as it is one of the time-honored ways that human beings across cultures and generations have made sense of their world and their immediate surroundings. In fact, every time we choose to communicate in spoken or written form, we are telling a story from our own viewpoint. At the start of every memo, proposal, speech, leaflet, flyer, brochure, web page, and newsletter article, we are in essence saying, "I want to tell you an important thing that will be of great interest you, the reader or listener, and it may even change your life for the better..." In this sense, public relations is all about telling stories, or framing narratives on behalf of organizations and their employees so that their stakeholders will understand them better and most importantly, enable them to understand what is in the organization's activities for them alone that will impact on their lives in some way for the better.

So what exactly is public relations?

Public relations exists in every aspect of life—whether we like it or not—and is continuously practiced by many people on a daily basis. We all intensify our good points and downplay our shortcomings. A child trying to please its mother; an employee trying to impress the boss; a sales executive trying to make a customer purchase something—they are all attempting to show themselves and their chosen topic in the best light. And collectively, countries, governments, companies, pressure groups, communities, and trade associations all do the same thing. It is a rare circumstance, indeed, when someone wants to put forward a bad impression.

Organizations are no different, of course. They all want to put their best foot forward, which is why public relations has become a fundamental building block of business, politics, and philanthropy. The public relations function is present in every organization, whether or not it is clearly defined, whether implemented internally or by a consulting firm.

Overall, there are three ways that public relations works:

- It can try to create an opinion or attitude where none exists
- It can seek to reinforce an existing opinion about an issue, person, or organization
- It can attempt to change an existing opinion

And the way it works is all about getting someone else to talk about you in the public domain across a range of communication channels—through third parties—who become your credible advocates.

Picture this scenario... Man A tells Woman B that he is a great person. Hmm, it may be true, but it sounds like bragging and is not totally credible. And this is the role of advertising. Imagine then, if Woman C enters the picture and tells Woman B that Man A is a great person. That is far more convincing; particularly if Woman A already trusts the judgment of Woman B.

Or what about another everyday situation—in a job interview John tells the prospective employer that he has good people skills and is a good communicator in most situations—that is advertising. But no savvy interviewer would take personal opinion on face value and would turn to a third party for an objective opinion before making a decision to either accept or reject John as a viable candidate for the job.

And that, in a nutshell, is what public relations can do. It aims to generate positive communication about your organization through credible advocates, to create, reinforce, or change opinions about a subject or an organization's *raison d'être* over time.

Acknowledgment of Achievement

This is the "Biggie"—the way we like to define the public relations process is as "Acknowledgment of Achievement." It is not just an acknowledgment of a corporate action—but rather of an action that has made a difference in a given community, such as a fuel company sponsoring a beach clean-up day or the launch of a company's successful share offering. Companies use public relations to get the message across to their relevant communities that they are doing good things in the best interests of all concerned and are consequently gaining favorable recognition for that. In essence, PR is all about good performance and justifiable acknowledgment in the public domain.

The legendary Harold Burson, founder of global PR consultancy Burson-Marsteller, talks about the way in which the industry has developed over the last 50 years—how it has moved from the question of "How do I say it?" to "What do I say?" and now, thank goodness, to, "What do I do?".

We know that talking is not enough; you have to prove you can take action and have a history of taking the right action, in the right place, at the right time, with the right people in order to create the right impact.

Whether we are a politician, celebrity, opinion leader, employee, charity worker, CEO, or a green group, we use public relations to inform and educate our stakeholders through effective engagement using various communication channels to outline what we are doing, what we represent, and why, in the hope that, for better or for worse, we will receive significant feedback on this. PR is based on interactive dialogue and is not a unidirectional form of communication. We enter into a conversation with many individuals and groups interested in the organization and not in an attempt to persuade them that they need us—but rather to invite them to enter into a conversation about what more we can do for them to fulfill needs and expectations.

Longevity and Sustainability of PR

Public relations does not offer any organization a "quick fix" in bolstering its reputation or mining the goodwill of stakeholders. Any change in attitudes, beliefs, or behavior, to be sustainable (or why bother doing it at all), must be executed over time—based on the gradual reinforcement of your position. The relationship of trust that organizations are aspiring to by engaging in public relations activities must be first gained, developed, and then nurtured over time. The intention behind any public relations activity then, is not just to make people aware that an organization exists, and to get them to understand what it does, but it should also engender a deeper affinity for the organization's aims, intentions, operations, products, and services by communicating ethical practices and recognizable values in the interest of sustaining mutually beneficial relationships in the short-, medium-, and long-term. As with any relationship worth investing in, you want it to last forever and be as amicable as possible.

Model PR

Having established that creating a harmonious relationship with your stakeholders is a critical goal; the next job of public relations is geared to ensuring corporate survival and prosperity in a competitive environment. So, the question is how do we actually achieve this? What can we pull out of the public relations toolbox to facilitate this?

As professional communicators, PR practitioners are in the business of crafting messages to present a winning argument to their stakeholders, and they have many communications tools at their disposal to assist in achieving this.

As public relations is a relative newcomer both in the professional world and on the university syllabus, it has borrowed concepts from sociology, management, marketing, psychology, and mass communications to build up a solid public relations theoretical toolkit as a way of informing and guiding practice to some degree.

In this sense, applied communication models such as Harold Lasswell's "who says what to whom and with what effect?" are a valid starting point, yet only present a linear view of PR, rooted in (Lasswell, 1958)[1] other simple one-way or basic sender/receiver communication models. The actual effect of mediated messages on receivers is still a matter of debate, and many practitioners ascribe to the view that the message is the main thing to focus on as it is more reassuring to believe that you are in control of your communication campaign in the hope that it will have the desired persuasive impact, rather than none at all.

But, as PR practitioners are in the business of communicating professionally, and as communication is not a one-way street—they must be audience-focused at all stages of planning and preparing the message.

The received wisdom in understanding how audiences decode messages depending on their ideological viewpoint and cultural expectations is useful for public relations practitioners, as this knowledge can avoid miscommunication or misunderstanding. The uses and gratifications that motivate media audiences, such as entertainment values and information-seeking behaviors, also provide useful insights for the public relations practitioner when choosing effective communication channels to ensure that their messages actually reach the right stakeholders, and in making sure that the message output causes the desired outcome, whether cognitive, affective, or behavioral—by impacting the mindset, emotions, and actions of our specifically targeted audience.

Equally useful for public relations are theoretical models such as the "Diffusion of Innovations" theory (Rogers, 2003)[2] outlining how people process data and adopt new ideas across time, cultures and social systems by following a staged path of awareness, interest, trial, evaluation, and adoption. Other communication models highlighting the cognitive, emotionally affected, and behavioral response required also provide insights into the mind of the prospect by showing how public relations messages can be crafted to have the desired effect in an awareness raising campaign for a new product launch, or when starting a new public health initiative for avian flu prevention, for example.

Every public relations effort—every brochure, annual report, web page, news release, product launch, and lobbying effort—is trying to grab the attention of, and engage the receiver. In the simplest terms, public relations is the persuasive communicative process of guiding people to accept an idea, attitude, or action using both reasoning and creative expression. This relationship is based on establishing agreement and acceptance predicated on common ground and trust.

So, anything that provides insights into the mindsets and affections of stakeholders is of benefit to the public relations effort. Armed with some notion of what persuasive communication is, and how it works in the public relations frame, when backed up with insightful stakeholder research, it should get us well on the road to a successful public relations campaign.

Locating Public Relations in the Asia Pacific Context

While the emergence of modern public relations in the United States, Europe, and Australia/New Zealand was rooted in the growth of private industry in the 1930s, public relations in Singapore, Hong Kong, and other former Asian colonies was founded by expatriate companies in the 1960s and the developing role of government spokespersons and in-house information departments in the 1950s. Other Asian countries such as China, Korea, and Vietnam, followed soon thereafter, although there is still some way to go before they are all operating on the same level playing field.

The Asia Pacific region comprises many different cultures, languages, and belief systems both between and within the various nations, and this diversity clearly represents a challenge to the PR professional trying to communicate with stakeholders inside, outside, and across these national barriers.

Communications can break down at any stage of a campaign resulting in a distortion of the PR message due to a variety of factors including cultural differences, linguistic misunderstandings, information overload, or time constraints. The public relations industry is littered with apocryphal tales of PR failures due to cultural misunderstandings. There's the one about the East Coast US firm issuing a news release to launch their new IT product across Asia and in doing so, they employed a translator who used traditional Chinese script and literal ancient Chinese language. The over-complex language and pedantic style fell on the deaf ears of most of the Chinese-speaking Asian populations, thereby rendering the PR campaign meaningless and a waste of time and money.

It seems clear that if PR is based on the communication of positive messages about an organization's rationale, and is intent on building consensual relationships, then doing public relations in Asia requires knowledge of, and an empathy with, the varieties and vagaries of the multilayered, multicultural landscapes across the region. In economically developed nations in Europe and North America, the focus of PR activity centers on how public and private sector organizations communicate with key stakeholders. While this is also true of many Asia Pacific countries such as Australia, New Zealand, Japan, and Hong Kong, for example, PR for many nations in Asia Pacific resides in developmental programs powered by national governments and NGO or agencies mobilizing local communities on a variety of issues such as health, and is geared to advancing socioeconomic conditions.

Given that the culture of a society will determine the ways in which people communicate both verbally and non-verbally, public relations professionals operating in these geographical contexts must be mindful of the cultural and communicative nuances, whether they are facilitating internal communication between a new CEO and employees, or externally repositioning an organization in the minds of consumers, green groups, government officials, and investors.

We note that most critiques by practitioners and scholars alike on the subject of public relations apply a Western communication model in framing public relations activities—which is clearly only part of the picture in an Asian Pacific context. It is our intention to walk the PR talk and more accurately redraw the public relations universe to include a real Asia Pacific perspective. This will more accurately reflect the realities of public relations practice in the region. Without a doubt, and based on our own working experience, we cannot just head for the filing cabinet or the computer file and pick out a generic, universal PR solution for those wanting to develop meaningful stakeholder relations in any locality—although it would appear that often this is the direction of most books written on the subject, while also being the habit of some practitioners.

James Grunig and Todd Hunt[3] provide a useful model that charts the evolution of public relations and which is relevant to the growth and application of public relations throughout the region. This theoretical/practical construct consists of four sections including: (1) the propaganda oriented press agency/publicity model based on one-way communication used by governments in evolving economies and product promoters in developing countries; (2) the public information model of truthful one-way communication typified by non-profit organizations, local government departments, and some small businesses; (3) the two-way asymmetric model comprising an interactive, yet imbalanced communication flow in favor of the sender as practiced by most competitive businesses and political campaigning; and (4) the two-way symmetric model or public relations "ideal" scenario based on two-way balanced communication resulting in mutual understanding and equality as used by regulated organizations throughout Asia Pacific.

These are clearly abstracted representations of public relations reality, originally Western-centric, and are not mutually exclusive in application as they seem to suggest. Yet, they are useful models for demonstrating the range of possible public relations approaches in theory and practice and the varying relationships between practitioner and publics in the persuasive communication process. However, the model presented next represents the Asia Pacific communications universe more accurately.

Asia Pacific Model

Public relations is fundamentally about managing relationships based on good communication that fosters mutual understanding and a demonstration of need fulfillment. The "one size fits all" PR mentality will not work globally—let alone across the differing markets in Asia. We suggest a reworking of our assessments and assumptions about stakeholder insights based on a realization that the Asian stakeholder comes from a unique cultural base and, as such, what they are looking for in life, and how they will fulfill their aspirations and needs can be different from other parts of the world and should be taken into account.

Much work by cross-cultural specialists has noted the basic cultural differences between the Asian collectivist cultures—where group ties and hierarchical relationships are paramount in contrast to the supposedly more individualistically oriented Western cultures, which aspire to self-fulfillment and individual achievement. Essentially, we are all searching to fulfill goals, dreams, and desires. Depending on our stage of social and economic development according to sociologist Abraham Maslow's hierarchy of needs model (see Figure 1.1), on a sliding scale of needs we go from craving physiological survival based needs, through the desire for safety, social acceptance, and self esteem to the ultimate level of being—self-actualization or the "I did it my way" principle. Basically it's a way of saying the more we have, the more we desire, which is the consumer manifesto writ large.

We can build on this notion of motivators that drive our stakeholder's lives by reworking Maslow's model. In this way, we can develop a more useful understanding of Asian stakeholders for public relations purposes

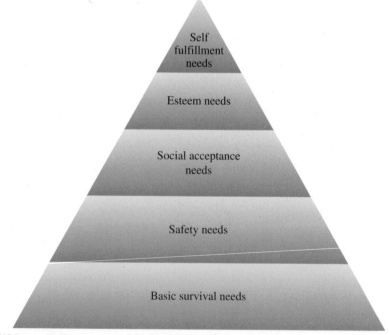

FIGURE 1.1 Maslow's Hierarchy of Needs[4]

and develop the content of our key communications messages accordingly by focusing on values more pertinent to the local culture, as shown in our diagrammatic representation. Here, progression up the needs pyramid is reworked to reflect more authentic, localized cultural motivators.

If in Western cultures the individual's needs of power, success, and self-fulfillment are dominant, in the Asian context, the social needs of affiliation, admiration, and status can often be more compelling. Hence these values are positioned at the center of the Asian communications universe in the model (see Figure 1.2). This means that the collectivist social self in the Asian context frequently dominates the individualistic private self and is the prime motivator for decision making. In this context, the public relations professional should articulate more collectivist wants and affiliations in public relations messages in order to connect with stakeholders in a more relevant and engaging manner. So, for example, if you were launching a government-funded program in the region to make people more environmentally responsible by recycling all of their household waste, the key message would focus on everyone's responsibility as part of a community effort to develop community ownership of the idea. In addition, a campaign to raise AIDS awareness might illustrate the problem and its prevention by using groups of local HIV positive patients to tell their stories or a use a local celebrity to endorse it. The caveat is of course that as countries and societies develop, their need priorities may change and a downturn in

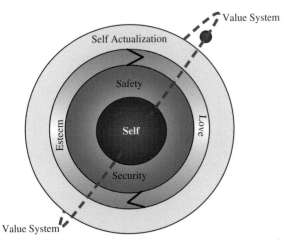

FIGURE 1.2   Devereux & Peirson-Smith's Asia Pacific Communication Universe

the economy may also have an impact on both individual and collective aspirations. So, we might expect to see more developed countries in Asia shift from a focus on conspicuous consumption fuelled desires and habits to a concern with conserving resources. Yet, even if the priority for certain needs and motivations shift in response to environmental changes over time—the public relations professional, in communicating with stakeholders, has to be ever alert to those dynamics and be mindful of the local cultural nuances and how they fit into the global picture.

Endnotes

1. Lasswell, Harold. *Politics: Who Gets What, When, How* (Cleveland, Ohio: Meridian, 1958).
2. Rogers, Everett M. *Diffusion of Innovations.* 5th edition (New York: New York Free Press: 2003).
3. Grunig, J. E. and Hunt, T. *Managing Public Relations.* (New York: Holt, Rinehart & Winston, 1984).
4. Adapted from A.H. Maslow, *A Theory of Human Motivation* (1943). Psychological Review 50, pp. 370–396.

CHAPTER 2

Public Relations Strategy

Ask a person on the street what they know about public relations, and when pressed to talk about anything beyond vague notions of publicity and spin, they may bring to mind special events or stories they read in a newspaper. These are tactics, or the "what we do," to demonstrate how an organization is connected with and contributing to the community in which it operates. They are the visible outcome of the PR strategic planning process. The prudent planning, however, that preceded these public relations events will be the real determiner of how effective we have been in achieving the organization's communications objectives.

A Management Function

The strategic role for PR is based on the premise that its function is to manage communications for the organization's external and internal stakeholders to ensure that each understands the other. In other words, the strategic PR process facilitates a dialogue or interaction between the organization and its multiple audiences in order to communicate a positive message about the activities of the organization.

Public relations practitioners are now recognized as indispensable in their ability to provide strategic counsel to senior executives and take their place in the boardroom alongside the key senior organizational players responsible for fulfilling organizational objectives, achieving visibility, and maintaining the corporate competitive profile. The capacity to devise strategy is the intellectual talent that really sets public relations apart from the routine aspects of marketing communications, and the capacity to put this strategy into practice is the value-added aspect of public relations professionals.

Typically, this proactive approach to public relations on behalf of an organization will consist of the business communications plan underpinning the company's standing, the communications strategic program for employees and shareholders on all organizational levels, and the integrated marketing communications plan devised to promote the goods and services that the company produces to attract customers, stimulate sales, and fulfill business targets.

Actually, doing this or putting strategic visions into practice requires that the public relations practitioner plans an approach with almost military precision. There is a globally-recognized "blueprint" for developing a public relations program. It goes something like this:

1. Aims/Objectives—what do we want to achieve?
2. Analysis—what are the barriers or drivers to achieving these objectives?
3. Strategy—how are we going to do it?
4. Communication—how are we going to say it?
5. Implementation—what are we going to do?
6. Evaluation and Research—what was the impact and did we achieve our objectives?

A Worked Example

Let's now take a look at each one of these aspects of the PR strategic planning process so we can understand how they work. But before we start, there's a disclaimer to be made. Any model of this kind can only be a representation of reality and a not very accurate one at that, because no matter how descriptive or real it may seem, it cannot truly replicate the planning stages of a PR campaign. It is meant as a structured guide to approaching PR strategic planning. Also, despite the seeming linearity of this approach as it is articulated here—the application of the strategic PR approach in practice will be subject to constant review and updating as the actual campaign evolves to ensure that stakeholders' needs are fully accommodated at all points, and that assumptions and guesswork are cut to a minimum given the potential for miscommunication.

For the purpose of reviewing these blueprint elements, we will use two imaginary situations:

Scenario A

Fast Fashion Co., a European fashion brand, will launch in Hong Kong and Southern China amid strong local competition and two relatively new European entrants.

Scenario B

AsiaCom, a large telecommunications company, has to announce 10,000 redundancies in its factories and service centers across the Asia Pacific region due to the global economic meltdown and introduction of new equipment. Employees and union groups at various plants and centers across Asia are demonstrating in public against these layoffs and petitioning legislators.

1. Aims and objectives

At the heart of the PR strategic planning process lie two layers of objectives, as these tell us in clear and uncompromising terms what we want to achieve in the short-, medium-, and long-term through our public relations campaign efforts. They are, first, organizational or business objectives and, second, communications objectives, and the two sets of objectives must be aligned.

These objectives should be understandable and unambiguous so that everyone working with them in the organization, from senior management to the marketing team and beyond, understands what is to be achieved, so that they can be used as a reliable benchmark to determine the success of the public relations effort overall and over time.

The orientation of these objectives can be positive or negative depending on the specific situation. So, they could be framed positively to achieve something, or negatively to stop something from happening, or even to prevent a situation from getting worse.

In public relations, we cannot automatically assume a cause and effect scenario. Informing stakeholders in PR programs will not automatically lead to effective stakeholder relationships. Disseminating a PR message will not necessarily result in preferred changes in attitudes, awareness, and behavior. This clearly ignores the complexities of the persuasive communications process that public relations deals in.

We need to take a rational approach to setting business objectives for our programs, as we know there are many aspects of business that we simply cannot reach. For example, public relations cannot impact the price of oil, so we may never be able to satisfy some drivers. And, as we say in chapter 14, communication objectives also need to be fully grounded in reality. They need to be precise and measurable, so it is clear to see how far the results of the program have gone toward achieving the objectives. We should not overpromise or undersell. If we are too modest in our aims, then the results may imply that more could have been achieved.

Equally, if the aims are too ambitious in terms of what can be done, this will lead to disappointment among stakeholders.

Here are examples of good and bad objectives for our two scenarios:

These are poor business objectives:

- Launch Fast Fashion brand in Asia.
- Minimize the negative associations of the redundancies made by Asia-Com and restore positive image.

These are good business objectives:

- Initiate $1,000,000 in sales of Fast Fashion brand clothing among teenagers in Hong Kong and Southern China.
- Ensure uninterrupted business continuity and increase annual margin by 10 percent.

These are poor communication objectives:

- Raise the profile of new Fast Fashion brand among target markets in Hong Kong and China to create awareness.
- Raise awareness of the long-term benefits of the redundancies.

These are good communication objectives:

- Ensure that women aged 18 to 24 in Hong Kong and Southern China are exposed to positive messages about Fast Fashion 20 percent more often than last year.
- Ensure that all relevant stakeholders—including remaining employees, shareholders, unions, government officials, and key media—understand the reasons for the redundancies and the long-term benefits for the business and the community.

2. Research

To position our organization in the way it wants to be perceived, we need to do our homework in terms of where we are placed in the hearts and minds of our various and multiple stakeholders. The market research should initially determine;

- What our stakeholders—that is, those who have a stake in the organization as a customer or as an influencer—actually think and feel about the organization and how well its rationale is understood, through public opinion surveys, recall surveys, focus groups, media content analysis, and situational analysis
- Why stakeholders perceive the organization in a particular way

With this knowledge in place, it is possible to identify the public relations strategy that can address these knowledge and information gaps on behalf of the organization.

Organizations are looking for deliverable and demonstrable solutions to their communications-based problems in the sense that the challenge facing both public and private sector organizations is the need to establish and maintain visibility in the relevant marketplace by getting the right message out to the right people, at the right time, using the right channels, and getting the right response as a consequence.

The planning for this approach relies on the ability to think strategically based on an in-depth knowledge of the organization in relation to the competition and in terms of how you can communicate the difference and uniqueness of what it has to offer to various stakeholders.

The starting point of strategic planning for the public relations effort is a situational analysis to identify the issues that a company is facing and is concerned about in addition to the contextual background of those issues. The public relations professional will need to be immersed in every aspect of organizational activities as a preliminary to preparing the communications focused situational analysis. He or she should be conversant with the organization's overall business rationale, including the aspects of ownership, its position in the marketplace (scale, structure, and competitors), products and services that it produces, the specific target audiences, former and existing communications initiatives, budget available, and time frame of anticipated communications.

Typically, this situational analysis will kick off with a summary of the overall industry in which the organization is operating—locally, regionally, and globally—if relevant to the scale and scope of the organization. This might be followed by a profile of the organization itself and a SWOT (Stengths, Weaknesses, Opportunities, and Threats) analysis outlining its strengths and weaknesses in terms of its reputation and its brand position, how well-known it is, and what people are thinking about the organization.

SWOT ANALYSIS

- Strengths
- Weaknesses
- Opportunities
- Threats

The situational analysis frames the public relations communications campaign effort providing a framework to analyze the real issues that need to be fixed by implementing the strategic PR program. It ultimately tells us what the barriers to our success are and what could drive a good result.

3. Strategy

Public relations strategies are the next critical step to getting the job done. They outline the overall approach that you will take in order to position

---

Here are strategies for our examples:

Scenario A

Tap into the celebrity aspirations of the target market and their belief that US clothing is trendier than local clothing.

Scenario B

Demonstrate how the redundancies have to be made in order for the company to prosper in the current economy, continue to offer employment for millions of other employees, and provide its much-needed products to the community.

your organization and its products and services in the marketplace and how you will distinguish them from the competition. Strategies address both the rational and emotional—providing logical and affecting reasons for stakeholders to support the objectives.

It is easy to confuse strategies with tactics at this stage. However, all you have to remember is that strategies are the "how to do it" and the tactics are the "what we will actually do."

In order for the strategies to work, we need to be sure we are addressing the right audience. All good communication begins and ends with the target audience or stakeholders that must be reached in this staged process. They are the objective or vehicle for our public relations effort in that they can generate favorable opinion about the organization, reinforce existing positive opinion, or change negative or nonexistent opinion with the consequent changes in behavior—the ultimate goal of the persuasive PR effort. We need to reach them, provide new information, persuade them to look at the organization in a different or new way, and have an impact on their behavior in how they interact with the organization.

Here are our examples of target audiences:

Scenario A

Targets – Fashion-savvy females and males between the ages of 16 and 24 in Hong Kong and urban China

Influencers – Peers, older sisters, mothers, fashion media, and Fast Fashion retail assistants

Scenario B

Targets – Employees, customers, shareholders, suppliers, local community, and, possibly, industry regulators

Influencers – Labor organizations, government officials, politicians, industry organizations, analysts, financial regulators, academics, and the business and news media

Building Sustainable Stakeholder Relationships

Go to the people
Live with them
Learn from them,
Love them.
Start with what they know,
Build with what they have.
But with the best leaders
When the work is done
the task is accomplished
The people will say,
"We have done this ourselves."

Lao Tzu, Chinese philosopher and poet, Tao Te Ching

The relational aspect of public relations activity cannot be underestimated. Building and maintaining relationships with groups or stakeholders— be they employees, government officials, journalists, investors, or local communities—is critical to an organization's competitive survival. This relationship-building activity lies at the heart of the strategic public relations effort as a means of enabling stakeholders as interested parties to better understand who you are, what you do, why you do it, and what your relationship with them is. You need to get full stakeholder commitment to your cause and *modus operandi*, but this can only be achieved effectively and in a sustained way by demonstrating the purpose and value of the organization and its outputs to those people who matter and who care.

The typical modern organization is faced with many critical publics whom it must communicate with frequently and directly.

Every organization, irrespective of size and function must be sensitive to the self-interests, desires, and concerns of each *identifiable* stakeholder group. We must get inside the heads, hearts, and skins of our stakeholders to truly understand them by pinpointing and further negotiating their perceptions of our organization.

Prioritizing Stakeholders   To drive forward targeted public relations activity on each PR project or campaign, we have to choose the stakeholders whom we want to focus on for the particular communication objectives concerned.

Case Study

In Korean, *Sebaro*, the name of the government's budget misuse reporting center means, "to use tax revenue rightly, properly, and correctly," which is a directive that aligns with the Korean Ministry of Planning and Budget's operational brief to deploy the tax revenue as a major source of the national budget in an appropriate and efficient way. The tax scheme was beset by public apathy toward the system of having to report the government's inefficient use of personal tax revenues, regarded as a waste of time. Negative perceptions about Sebaro's work were also heightened by the fact that only 10 percent of the 2,000 claims files were actually legitimate.

Looking for a long-term change in attitudes and behavior to generate future responsible citizens, the campaign purposely targeted young people aged 10-30 years old.

A more relaxed, fun approach to the campaign was adopted than the more traditional, serious public affairs format given the youth demographic being pinpointed. The concept adopted for the whole campaign was "treasure hunting." This theme was encapsulated in a cartoon icon representing a typical citizen looking through a telescope to scrutinize the government's tax usage and budgetary policy.

By inviting over 100 participants to a Sebaro Youth Camp, the campaign team aimed to activate the interest of the targeted youth demographic. Here, they gained specialist training on economic and citizenship issues, in addition to team building and presentations skills issues.

An online cartoon series was launched across 60 websites featuring the Sebaro icon in Flash animated form, backed up by nursery song style music. This offered an involving way of engaging with concepts such as budget waste reduction, valid reporting methods, plus the advantages and means of protection for citizen's filing complaint reports.

Finally, Sebaro was used as a question in a favorite TV quiz program, while the campaign widened its target to the middle-age demographic by using credible, third-party endorsements.

Source: Asia Pacific PR Awards 2008.

Clearly, we can't communicate with all of our stakeholders all of the time. Selectivity is called for here. Not everyone can be invited to the "public relations party" as it won't always be "their scene." One method of identifying the relevant stakeholder is to conduct an audit of the environment in which the organization operates, listing all of the possible people and groupings who are important to the organization. Having identified the macro universe of existing and potential stakeholders with whom the

Case Study

UPS launched the first-of-its-kind annual business monitor (ABM) in 2005 as a unique pan-regional survey highlighting competitive business issues confronting SMEs (small to medium sized enterprises) across Asia. This provided an opportunity for UPS to make connections with SME groupings across the region.

As ABM entered its fourth year of operation, the idea was to provide more tangible benefits to SMEs across the region as they faced a deteriorating economic climate.

UPS achieved this aim by repositioning ABM 2008 as a beacon to guide SMEs through the troubled waters of the difficult economic situation ahead.

UPS took the helm on dialogue with a range of local SMEs holding press conferences presented by UPS executives in 12 pan-Asian markets on this issue and detailing how SMEs could prepare for their future in these challenging times.

Further high-level meetings around the same theme were held in Thailand, Malaysia, and the Philippines, while in Taiwan there was an online launch of ABM 2008 including e-letters being dispatched to subscribers. Also, almost 15,000 ABM 2008 booklets were sent out in five languages to SMEs across the region.

This program enabled UPS to successfully reposition ABM into the premier guide providing direction and advice for SMEs and their stakeholders such as government and business agencies.

In addition to the original campaign brief, ABM operates as a business-to-business navigation tool. Inside two months of the ANB 2008 launch, over 215 media stories, with in excess of 100 million media impressions were created throughout the Asian region.

Source: Asia Pacific PR Awards 2008.

organization needs to communicate, these groupings can then be further subdivided, for example, based on their physical relation to the company—external (clients, legislators, journalists, community groups) or internal (existing and potential employees). Or, we could usefully divide our stakeholder group into two units—the primaries who enable us to fulfill our business objectives and the secondaries who will influence the former to affect a positive business result. More complex stakeholder categorizations can also be used (see box below).

This type of categorization, based on stakeholder perceptions as a window into their attitudinal responses to the organization, is important and is a critical component of the PR homework that needs to be done before the strategic planning commences.

To See Ourselves as Others See Us...   Knowledge about the perceptions held by stakeholder groups related to the organization from formal surveys or informal interviews will provide invaluable insights into where the organization is located in relation to its allies and opponents—supporters, neutrals, and antagonists. This data in turn will enable the strategic public relations plan to be carefully honed, based on how and what is needed to be factored into the public relations program.

GRUNIG AND REPPER (1992) IDENTIFIED ACTIVE "PUBLICS" VS. PASSIVE "PUBLICS"[1]

Active—seek out information and respond to organizational initiatives—more likely to affect an organization

Passive—do not proactively want to engage with the organization

Latent—only become active when they are prompted by a particular stimulus

---

PR practitioners need to know what stimuli will trigger a reaction among these publics (or stakeholders) so they can use the right communication at the right time in order to make latent and passive stakeholders into more active and involved partners of the organization (Grunig and Repper (1992).

Hallahan (2000)[2] believes that the traditional publics theory overemphasizes active publics at the expense of inactive groups. He focuses on the role of both knowledge and involvement with an issue or organization before activism takes place.

HALLAHAN'S THEORY OF STAKEHOLDERS

Aware—high knowledge, low involvement

Active—high knowledge, high involvement

Aroused—low knowledge, high involvement

Inactive—low knowledge, low involvement

Non-publics—no knowledge, no involvement

4. Communicating the message

Devising the message lies at the heart of the strategic public relations program. The notion of alignment is also critical here as the message should be consistent across all of the media channels chosen to disseminate it—leaflets, flyers, brochures, posters, speeches, news articles, news releases, features, op-eds, annual reports, blogs, and websites to name a few.

The Power of Three...   Some say that "two's company and three is a crowd," but in public relations, as with all promotional communications, three is a magical and powerful number when it comes to conveying your message to the audience. Scientific evidence suggests that the left side of the human brain, responsible for logical knowledge processing, craves structure and retains information more effectively when it is packaged in this quantity. Three is a manageable number for recall purposes. If you add more messages and information, you are likely to create an overload situation. Your audience will not recall what you have said or, only very little, and your program will be in danger of being off track.

There are various ways of developing and messages; in PR you will hear about message houses, message blocks, and even messaging umbrellas. A message is the one thing you want people to remember—something that will impact the way they think about you and act toward you.

An important thing to remember is that messages are made up of both rational and emotional reasons. All the facts in the world will not change an already strong opinion; there has to be an appeal to the emotional psyche. At the same time, a completely emotional message with no factual backing is doomed to failure as well.

Thus, a message has to be both aspirational and believable. Without tangible evidence to back it up, then it will have little impact. For example, it is one thing to say you are the largest company in your industry; you need to prove it as well. If you want to apologize for an error, you will need to back it up with proof of that emotion through action.

One area of frustration in working with corporations is a tendency to mix up messages and facts. Saying that you are the largest company in the industry is a fact or proof point; the message is the consequence or benefit of being the largest company; such as trust in its financial strength and the ability to take on large orders

There are two broad categories of messages that can be created—corporate and brand messaging; and issues and crisis messaging. Over the years, the public relations industry has developed a template guide on how to craft these types of messages, as outlined below:

Brand or corporate messages:

Message One: what the market environment needs

Message Two: what your organization or product can offer to fulfill that need

Message Three: a point of differentiation, why your organization or product can fulfill the need better than anyone else

Issues messages:

Message One: frame the actual issue and its impact

Message Two: what is currently being done to address the issue

Message Three: the broad perspective; what might happen if the issue is not addressed or how others are addressing the issue successfully

Crisis messages:

Message One: the concern

Message Two: actions that are being taken or will be taken to resolve the crisis and support the victims

Message Three: the context in which the crisis is taking place; for example, it may be a freak accident after a long safety record

Here are our examples:

Scenario A - Brand and Corporate Messages:

Message One: Young women in Hong Kong and Southern China want to wear trendy and up-to-date fashion from the US, at affordable prices

Message Two: Fast Fashion is the number one clothing store in the US, which specifically makes affordable clothing for the 16 to 24 year age range

Message Three: Fast Fashion's collection has been designed by world famous, US model, Miss X

Scenario B – Issues Messages:

Message One: The economic crisis is having a major impact on our business, decreasing sales and increasing costs

Message Two: We are sad to make these redundancies but need to do so in order to allow the company to survive

Message Three: We are one of several companies in our industry making these redundancies in order to continue operating and supplying our services

5. Implementation—the tactics

The tactics are the ways and means of putting the public relations strategy into practice—the "what we will do." They are not to be confused with strategies, otherwise we would be putting the cart before the horse.

Here are our examples:

Scenario A – A Potential Tactic:

Invite Miss X to host a fashion show and media conference in Guangzhou to introduce the collection to invited stakeholders and the media, in order to generate word-of-mouth communication and media coverage in our target publications.

Scenario B – A Potential Tactic:

Hold a one-on-one briefing for the CEO with an influential journalist to outline the rationale behind the redundancies, in order to generate a thoughtful and positive article on the redundancies and long-term business plan for AsiaCom.

The tactics will be pulled from a wide range of activities in our public relations toolbox, and you can read about them in the following chapters.

Timing   Timing is essential. Not only the overall timing of the program, but also the day-to-day clock watching to make sure your news story does not arrive too late for publication or broadcast deadline or was already reported on yesterday and is old, redundant news. There are no second chances in the business of generating news.

So, a carefully crafted timeline for the duration of the program, detailing each proposed activity or tactic from media releases to event launches, in terms of when it will occur and how long it will run, is essential as a visual representation of the public relations program.

Hint: start at the end point of the program and work backward to ensure that you fit each public relations activity into the time frame so that it is workable in the time available, be it 12 months or 12 days.

Nothing in life goes completely to plan and certainly not when you are dealing with highly volatile variables such as human beings and their fickle changes of ideas, feelings, and behaviors. To be realistic we have to recognize that a strategic public relations plan is just that—a planned way of doing something. As such, it should be open to flexible interpretation as events unfold, and monitored and adjusted as the PR program evolves organically to ensure that it is tailored to specific needs and responsive to unforeseen developments as the campaign is implemented.

6. Measurement and evaluation

And so we come to the final stage, evaluating our success. But not here... turn to chapter 14 instead.

Endnotes

1. Grunig, J. E. and Repper, F. C. "Strategic Management, Publics and Issues." *In: Excellence in Public Relations and Communications Managment.* J. E. Grunig ed. (Hillsdale, New Jersey: Lawrence Erlbaum Associates Inc., 1992).
2. Hallahan, (2000) *Inactive Publics The Forgotten Publics in Public Relations* Public Relations Review, Volume 26, Issue 4, Winter 2000 pp. 499–515.

CHAPTER 3

Connecting with the Media

> - Major daily newspapers carry 150–250 stories each day
> - Television news broadcasts have 15–20 stories for each 30 minutes of broadcast
> - Radio broadcasts can have 5–15 news stories for each news bulletin (3–5 minutes in length)
> - Magazines can carry 50–1,000 stories for each magazine

In chapter 2, we looked at messaging as part of strategic planning for public relations. The way in which we deliver messages across any medium can mean the difference between winning and losing the communication battle. If delivered well, they can win acclaim for our product or position on an issue, but if delivered poorly, they can generate a damaging image that could plague an organization for years to come.

While there are, of course, many different types of channels for messages, the credible and influential news media—be they print, broadcast, or online—remain key channels for the public relations industry.

This chapter looks at the all-important relationship between the public relations profession and the media, and how they can effectively communicate with each other.

The Media and Democracy

It is common parlance to say that the media are an essential part of democracy. Democracy belongs to "the people," but it can only work well if "the people" are well informed. The media's job is to inform them. The Fourth Estate, as the media is sometimes called, is entrusted with the mission of ensuring that the people have access to a diverse range of views and ideas.

But how does this work in the Asia Pacific region, where not all governments follow the traditional model of democracy as practiced in Europe and the United States? In markets such as Mainland China, Vietnam, and Cambodia, the media's most important role is to communicate the policies and views of the government. Even in democratic markets such as Malaysia and South Korea, where the media are effectively independent, they will typically take a pro-state approach and will always be looking for news that shows benefit to their country.

The Asia Pacific domestic media can be daunting at first look from the outside. Not only do we have to deal with the differences between countries' culture and language; but we also have to take into account the distinct variations within countries: India's many ethnic groups; Singapore's multi-cultural society; Hong Kong's bipolarity between independence and the motherland.

However, even in the most pro-government newspapers in China, there is still substantial commercial news, which reports on both domestic and international enterprises. And, although the bias and amount of coverage can be largely dictated by public policy, journalists in Asia Pacific will respond and react to the same methodologies employed in "the West." They are still looking for news in a timely fashion, for commentary from experts, and for access to trends and data. So, while we need to tread carefully among the cultural and political differences, we can also employ largely the same techniques used elsewhere in the world.

An undervalued role

There was a time when public relations was synonymous with media relations. If we wanted to reach our audience, we first had to reach the media. Many observers still regard working with the media as the only role of public relations. PR professionals, however, know it is only one part of a strategic communications program, but recognize that it still forms a key element in the repertoire, and building mutually respectful relationships with the media remains a critical part of that effort.

As recently as the end of the 1990s, the ability to know and understand the media was regarded as a vital element of any professional's role. However, as the PR profession has evolved to a more strategic level, the ability to work with the media has decreased. Looking at the websites of some of the top public relations firms in the world, only two of them list media relations as a capability at all. Yet what do most organizations want—they want media coverage. And why not? Media results are instantly tangible and can have quick results. There is a danger that our profession will forget to employ the basics, as it grapples with the digital era and new corporate practices.

The media landscape is also changing, and the impact of digital technology on our profession is discussed in detail in chapter 12. The opportunities for print media coverage overall have shrunk because the number of outlets has decreased, owed in part to a dramatic fall in advertising revenues. Although print opportunities have been reduced, the number of online publications and news outlets has increased. And, of course, many traditional print publications are offering content online.

It is true that the Internet has made everyone a reporter and a publisher. However, we would contend that the growing world of blogs is bolstering the media, not undermining it, as many feared. There is simply too much to take in with all the websites, blogs, and news forums, and we still rely on the filtering system of the news media to make the news digestible and ensure third-party credibility.

Public relations' ability to act as a source and even a subsidy for the media remains as important in the digital age as it has always been. The number of online media outlets has grown substantially and, as a consequence, the number of reporters at each outlet has also been reduced. Therefore, journalists' resources are constrained, which results in a greater reliance on public relations as a reliable source for news.

DON'T PRESS YOUR LUCK

You will note that we use the word "media" in this book, not "press." Press only refers to the print medium, and does not include broadcast or digital media. Although it is common practice to use the word "press" in some countries, it is incorrect, so we will use the word "media" throughout this book.

So What is Media Relations?

An old-fashioned view of media relations was that it was all about "managing" relations with the media—be they reporters, editors, or producers. It is hard to imagine a journalist being delighted to be "managed." A better definition is to talk about the cultivation of a good relationship between the media and an organization. The result of these relationships is, hopefully, that the public relations professional gets fair and accurate reporting of their story; while the reporter has a valuable source of timely and accurate information and ideas.

Working effectively with the media requires a good understanding of the many types of outlets and their differences. Each aspect of the media—be it news, business, lifestyle, medical, travel, technical industry—has a different audience and often, a slightly different vision of what makes a story.

Similarly, the view of a domestic reporter in, say, Jakarta, will differ from that of a *Wall Street Journal Asia* reporter. We need to understand the agenda of each reporter to ensure our messages are hitting their mark. This may mean adapting the communication content we deliver—changing the emphasis, and adding or omitting details.

Hack vs. flack—love at first sight?

The relationship between a journalist and a public relations professional is ambiguous at the best of times. It is common to hear the older generation of journalists (the hacks) disparage the public relations professional (the flacks). On the other hand, perhaps because of the increase of the professionalism of the public relations industry, most of the "younger" generation of journalists have grown up with the public relations industry around them and appreciate its input.

At its best, the relationship between a journalist and public relations professional is symbiotic. However, you cannot rely on contacts alone. If you do not have a good story, all the connections in the world will not get your story published.

What are the media really like?

Developing and nurturing ongoing media relationships requires that you understand and respect what journalists work lives are like. While they can seem all powerful and influential (and sometimes are)—they are also under pressure to produce a good story and to produce one to deadline. No wandering away from the computer just because they're lost for words. They need to write it now.

Journalists are also employees. And they are employed by businesses who, guess what, want to make money. While there are a number of free news services around, including public and government media, most media we deal with are commercial enterprises. They have to produce content which interests their readers, which in turn generates advertising dollars from companies who want to talk to those readers.

Finally, while the media in a democratic society are supposed to be unbiased and fair, it would be unnatural for journalists not to have their own opinion. It is also hard for a journalist to ignore the political slant of the publisher. Certainly, bias does exist in the media all over the region. That said, except in the case of national agendas, the vast majority of journalists aim to be objective and fair in their reporting. If bias does occur, it is most likely accidental, or simply a factor of not being able to obtain information about the other side of the issue.

A Note on Gratuities

The large majority of journalists and public relations practitioners around the world say it is not professional for media to accept payments from news sources in return for coverage. If the media are accepting payment, then it is impossible for them to remain independent.

Back in the early 1990s, a group of public relations consultancies working in Mainland China, including Burson-Marsteller and Ogilvy PR Worldwide, joined with some of the major international corporations to agree that no one would pay a fee any more to a reporter for coverage. The only gratuity that was permissible was to cover travel expenses. This sounds like an odd exceptional clause, but it was based on the then small salary earned by journalists who were also expected to pay their own way on public transport to reach a media event, which sometimes limited their mobility if their cashflow was poor. It is hard to say how rigorously this agreement was enforced at the time, but there is no doubt it paved the foundations for the outlawing of bribes and gratuities within the media in China.

Despite the good news from China, it is, unfortunately, still commonplace in some countries to pay a gratuity or travel expense. However, as the region becomes more developed, we can hope this practice will die out in time.

A Recipe for News

One of the first steps in developing a media relations program is to understand what exactly is regarded as news by your target audience, and which media is most likely to carry the news. That done, you then need to know which section or program is most suitable. There is no point trying to place a story on the benefits of health food in the business section of a newspaper.

There are many ways to generate news. For example, we can issue a report, make a prediction, mark an anniversary, launch a new product, open a new building, conduct a poll or survey, lead a protest, create an award, stage a special event, organize a tour, or appoint an important person. You get the picture.

Thus, it goes without saying—we hope—that any news story needs to have sufficiently interesting information to grab a reporter's attention. To make the news palatable, however, there are three more important ingredients:

- *Timeliness*—the information needs to be new or be tied to an important date
- *Proximity*—the news should be related to the readership, either by geography or interest
- *Prominence*—the news should be about someone or something which is important to the readers

Once you have mixed these ingredients together, you just need to add the seasoning—your news should:

- come from credible sources,
- be confirmed by third parties, and
- be substantiated by facts.

When completed, the last step is to determine how you will communicate your news. The remainder of this chapter looks at some of the most commonly used "tools of the trade."

Media Releases

Often called news releases, media releases are the favored way businesses and organizations choose to tell the media about their news. However, with literally thousands of media releases arriving in the inbox of editors each day, we need to ensure that our release grabs attention and does not automatically end up in the e-mail recycle bin.

Given that most reporters work in a rushed and stressful newsroom environment, a tried and tested formula has evolved over the years, which helps reporters locate information fast. With just a quick scan, the editor can find out who sent the news, when it was issued, and what the main story is.

The formula is simple—each release needs to contain, in any order, $5 \times W + 1 \times H$, that is:

Who—is doing this or who is it happening to?

What—are they doing?

When—did they do this, or when will they be doing this?

Where—did it take place?

Why—did they do it?

How—did they make it happen?

Much has been said in recent years about the format of media releases and how they should be adapted to suit the digital age. This includes the importance of including hyperlinks, RSS codes, and keywords. Quite right too—the profession needs to ensure it is delivering information in the way reporters want to receive it. However, when it comes to changing the flow of information in media releases, we have our doubts. What could be simpler than giving the most important information up front, and backing this up with credible facts and data?

Given that we only have one or two pages to tell our complete story— unless it involves complex financial results—it is useful to adhere to a standard format, as follows. Note: in this chapter, we are concerned with content rather than the visual look of the release, which will vary between organizations.

1. Identification of Organization   It sounds obvious, but it is all too easy to send out a media release by e-mail and forget to include the company logo.

2. Media Release Identifier   We need to let the reporters know it is a media release, and not an advertisement.

3. Dateline and Placeline   Using the ingredients of timeliness and proximity, the release should let the reporters know when the information is being released—the dateline—and where it has been released—the placeline. The latter's importance is sometimes overlooked but, for example, a reporter in Hong Kong is more likely to be interested in news coming out of Hong Kong than, say, Tokyo.

4. Headline   The headline quickly summarizes the news in your release. It is probably one of the most important format elements in your release since the reporter might not even read the rest of the release if they are not interested after seeing the headline. Headlines should ideally be short and snappy, and use verbs in the present tense. Unless you are very creative and know the reporter has a sense of humor, it is best to avoid being too clever in the headline; that's the job of the sub-editor.

Some media releases use sub-headings to provide additional material which supports the main idea. However, they are optional.

5. Lead   This is where the reporter, editor, or producer looks to understand your news story in a nutshell. It should tell them exactly what the news is—using the $5 \times W + 1 \times H$ formula. Leads are vitally important because, after the headline, they give the reader the first indication of the topic and will determine if the reporter will think it worth their while to read on.

6. Main Body   These paragraphs work through the facts of your story in order of importance. Each paragraph in the body of the release should tell a story in itself by stating the main point first, explaining the purpose, and providing extra facts to support the point.

7. Quotations   Quotations from spokespeople or influencers provide emphasis to a point and give the news more credibility and also make the release more readable. However, public relations professionals need to ensure these quotations are new information, and not just a repetition of previous material covered in the release.

8. Boilerplate and Safe Harbor   At the end of the release, most organizations tack on a "boilerplate" description of whom and what they are. It is a standardized, brief description of the organization which appears in all media releases. The boilerplate normally includes the year the organization was founded, its area of expertise, product line or service, and its unique or most well-known characteristics. The information in the boilerplate is rarely used by the reporter, but it is an important part of the ingredient "prominence," demonstrating how important or relevant the organization is to the audience.

The boilerplate may contain some legalese, sometimes known as "safe harbor," which essentially says that any information or predictions given should not be used as a guarantee that the predictions will be met. This is important for publicly-listed companies to protect them from potential legal action or regulatory censure if the actual results differ from the company's expectations.

9. End and More   Before e-mail, it was common to mail or fax a media release to the media, which opened up the possibility that a page may get misplaced. For that reason, media releases over one page in length generally have the word "– more –" at the bottom of the first page or—1 of 2—to indicate there is more to come. With whole documents now sent as attachments, the chance of pages getting lost is greatly reduced. However, it is a sensible practice to continue, as is adding the word "end" to indicate the release is concluded.

10. Contact Details   Details of whom the reporter can contact for more information are vital, as is giving a sufficient option of telephone numbers to call; particularly if the reporter has questions outside of office hours. Contact details may be at the top of a media release or at the end, depending on corporate style. In Asia Pacific, it is commonplace to have more than one contact person; particularly if working across different geographies and time zones.

The style

When writing a media release, remember to just present the facts and do not attempt to editorialize—avoid superlatives and "puffery" where possible. The shorter, sharper, and more factual a release is, the greater its chances of being published. In addition, presenting the release in the editorial style of the target publication will also increase its chances of being used by the editor.

Given the needs of reporters and easier access to information, it is important to format the media release so it can be easily found during an Internet search. Search engine optimization, social bookmarking, and RSS are discussed in chapter 12. Reporters also find it useful if you add hyperlinks to online sources, where they can find more information or, perhaps, download images.

Photographs

A picture is worth a thousand words, and there is no doubt that a well set-up photograph, which fits the style of the publication, will greatly enhance your news.

You may decide to hold an official **photo opportunity** (photo op)—essentially the same as organizing a media conference (next section) but focused on providing photographers with an opportunity to capture a spectacular, interesting, or newsy image.

Key to a photo opportunity is the fact that it is designed to be visual only (photographed or filmed for broadcast). No statement will be read, no questions answered (or very few if it is a red carpet event)—and it should be completed in less than an hour.

Of course, you should only hold a photo op when you have something visual. Groups of men in business suits will not interest the media (unless they are heads of government). They are looking for unusual settings—be they business related or simply quirky; children, animals, and celebrities—not necessarily in that order—can enhance a photograph.

Useful tips for photography:

- Set up an area just for photographers—you may need to build a set of risers so they can all fit into the area and not be jostling for position. Sometimes, they bring ladders themselves, but they appreciate whatever you can provide. Where possible, you may like to separate the still photographers from the cameramen, as they will be looking for different shots.

- Ensure that any people taking part in the shot hold their pose, and repeat as many times as is necessary.

- Try to keep the "unknown" person away from the famous person, as the media will only want to see the celebrity; unless of course, the unknown is your CEO.

- At the event, provide the names and titles of all participants in the photograph; even describing physical appearance or dress if you think that will help the identification.

- Have as much branding as you can. Organizations are finally recognizing that a single logo or event name on a backdrop is likely to be cropped from any image. Instead, adopt the same approach as sporting events, and build a backdrop filled with your logo.

Still photographs

Most news, however, is not likely to require the presence of photographers, and a separate image will be sent along with the media release.

Asia Pacific was far ahead of the United States and Europe in its early adoption of color photographs. As recently as the early 1990s, the media in the United Kingdom, for example, would only accept black and white photographs or color transparencies. And pity the poor junior executive who stuck the caption on the back too tightly. However, in markets such as Singapore and Hong Kong, the media were already accepting color prints by this time and scanning them for use.

Images are all given in digital format now—the only issue is to ensure that the photograph file is of high-enough resolution, but not so large that it sinks your e-mail system. Also, you need to consider the orientation—check your target newspaper, magazine, or website to see what type of format they prefer—horizontal or vertical. Often a photograph will be used simply because it fits a space.

Writing captions

The caption helps the reporter in telling the story. Captions should be able to stand-alone if not printed with the news release. They should describe the situation rather than the image, and clearly indicate who is who. Finally, as they essentially "capture a moment in time" they should be written in the present tense and pique the reader's interest.

Case Study

GBF Pte. Ltd. appointed GolinHarris in 2008 as its public relations partner for its fifth successive *Global Brand Forum* in Singapore, themed "Maverick Approach to Brand Building." A primary objective was to drive early registrations and publicize the celebrity speakers, one of whom included the world famous founder of Wikipedia, Jimmy Wales.

Media interviews were pitched to local, regional, and international media publications based in and outside of Singapore. Pre-event interviews with the celebrity speakers were conducted through telephone and e-mail, a challenging task because many of the foreign media being pitched did not see the relevance for them to run a story about a forum that was to be held in another country. Despite this challenge, through generating extensive media coverage in local and foreign print, broadcast, and online media, GolinHarris helped GBF achieve their target of 600 forum attendees despite the steep fee of S$3,500 charged per head. On-site at the forum, the GolinHarris team facilitated several simultaneous media conferences and one-to-one interviews for the eight celebrity speakers, and managed a media center catering to more than 120 media.

In addition to developing the PR strategy and executing it over five months, GolinHarris developed all the media communications covering news releases and background briefs for all the celebrity interviewees taking the local, regional, and international media interviews. Three media releases were issued, including a post event release and another, to announce Jimmy Wales as Global Brand Icon Award winner for 2008. CORUM Swiss Timepieces sponsored the award.

More than 168 media hits in print, online, and broadcast media were achieved with total PR value of S$65 million. Coverage included profiles in the *International Herald Tribune*, BBC Asia, CNBC Asia, and other leading local, regional, and international print, broadcast, and online media.

Source: GolinHarris.

Media Conferences and Briefings

A media conference—news conference—makes it possible to quickly disseminate information and opinions through the news media.

The most important element of a media conference is "hard" news. The most damaging impact on your relationship with a journalist would be to invite them to an event which they do not consider newsworthy or could have easily been communicated in a media release.

You are likely to hold a media conference or briefing when:

- You are launching a major business or CSR (corporate social responsibility) initiative, taking a new direction, or making a major shift in policy or strategy
- You have breaking news such as unveiling a major new product or relaunching one
- You are responding to a crisis situation
- The announcement requires simultaneous media disclosure, typically related to financial results, if it is a public company
- The news can only be told effectively by having spokespeople accessible to the media for questions
- A very important spokesperson is taking part in the announcement

A checklist for organizing a media conference:

1. Choosing the location, date, and time:

   Select a centrally located, easily accessible site for the media, unless a remote location is essential to the story, such as a factory or special venue.

   If possible, choose a Tuesday, Wednesday, or Thursday. Mondays are difficult to organize as much of the material preparation and media contact will need to be completed on the Sunday, with the inconvenience that causes. Similarly, avoid the day before, or day after a holiday, unless the media conference has a holiday news angle.

   The best time for a media conference varies from country to country but, overall, the media tend to go to work later in this region than they do in the United States or Europe. Thus, the best time will be from midday up until 5 p.m., when deadlines are being reached.

   Avoid scheduling your event on the same day as other major news events, such as elections, big sporting events, and other competitors' events and, for places like Hong Kong, on a Wednesday if your news may be impacted by decisions from the weekly legislative meeting.

2. Develop the messaging and decide on the spokespeople.

3. Issue an invitation to the media early enough to book a space in their diaries, but not so early that they forget about the event. Follow up on responses.

4. Develop the venue decoration, including signage and branding for photographs to be taken.

5. Develop the media release and media kit, and internal Q&As.

6. Rehearse the presentations and questions.

7. Make sure you have sufficient staff to handle the jobs on the day—registration, microphone, MC of the event, and so on.

8. Ensure good follow-up after the event, to answer media questions and provide more information, as required.

Point of View

"Some of my reporter friends half jokingly accused me of betraying my former profession as a broadcast journalist when I defected to being a Media Coach/Trainer. My response: 'What I'm merely doing is to give confidence to the spokesperson so that they are more likely to accept an interview request from a journalist, even though they anticipate tough questions from you!' My advice to company spokespersons: 'Don't let one potentially negative question get in the way of you telling a good story!'"

Linda Lee Communications Coach/Trainer Acewood Group

Media Interviews

Taking part in media interviews is part and parcel of the job description of any senior executive these days. The key to a successful interview is to ensure that the desired messages are actually communicated; it is not enough just to answer the journalist's questions. Conducting media interviews and taking part in media conferences and media trips is a highly skilled job, and the vast majority of spokespeople undergo training to hone their skills. This chapter does not deal with media skills training in depth, which would be a whole book in itself, but does cover some of the basics you need to know.

First of all, **preparation** is vital. Before taking part in a media interview, a spokesperson needs to understand why the interview is taking place; what does the interviewer want? Who is the journalist and what have they written about the subject and you previously. Will they be interviewing other organizations?

Second, **understand the type of coverage** you are likely to achieve. An interview for a print publication or website will likely take longer than one for broadcast. It will also allow you to emphasize various points and go back and correct information, if required. A TV or radio interview can, on the other hand, be as short as one to two minutes, so it is important to have your messages and "sound bites" ready. Also, for broadcast, you need to know if the interview will be recorded for later broadcast, or if it will go out live.

Third, **know your own objective**. What do you want to accomplish and what headlines would you like to achieve?

And, fourth, **anticipate all types of questions**. Determine what the basic questions will be and also the "nightmare" question. If you have had a problem in the past or are facing a potential issue in the future, you can be sure the journalist will ask about this.

Every person who takes part in media interviews or media conferences will have a slightly different style. This is important, as the media do not want to interview a "message machine," but rather an individual who has something unique to say. There are, however, a few fundamental techniques that anyone can use in this situation:

- **Always answer** the question. Unless you actually address a question, the journalist will not move on, and will continue to ask the question. If you do not want to spend a lot of time answering a question, then use the opportunity to **bridge** to a message. For example:

  "Yes, that is correct, but what is really important is…"

  "No, we did not do this. What we did do is…"

  "Yes, but let me put that into perspective…"

- When you have an important message or fact to give, **flag** this to the journalist. For example, say the words:

  "The most important thing to remember is…"

  "Let me leave you with one point…"

- *Listing* is a useful technique, particularly in broadcast interviews. Start a sentence by telling the journalist how many items you will talk about—and then nine times out of ten, they will let you talk about all of these items. For example:

  "There are three things we need to remember. First…"

  "The two most important reasons why this has occurred are…"

- A favorite ploy of journalists is to keep silent sometimes, in the hope that the spokesperson will feel he or she has to fill the gap; perhaps with information that they did not plan on releasing. *Do not* be tempted to *fill the dead air*; this is the journalist's job, not yours. *Never speak off-the-record*. Sure, there will always be some people who will tell you that they regularly give tip-offs to the media and often talk off-the-record to their favorite journalists. However, for us mere mortals, do not take the risk. Friendships and contacts often break when a reporter is under pressure to file his story or is convinced he has the chance to make his once-in-a-lifetime scoop.

- *Never use the words "no comment."* You might as well hold up a neon sign to tell the world that you are hiding something. Instead, offer an explanation why you cannot talk about this issue. For example:

  "I am sure you appreciate I cannot talk about this at present, as this is a legal matter. However…"

  "I am sure you appreciate that this is commercially-sensitive information, which I do not want to give to our competitors. However…"

  "I am sure you appreciate that we need to ascertain all the facts first. Our first priority is people's safety which is why we are…"

Media Kits

Media kits are the basic tool of public relations. These are packs of information distributed to journalists to help them write articles or produce broadcast items. They are typically used at large-scale media events such as media conferences, product launches, or given to journalists interviewing organization representatives.

The contents of a media kit will be entirely dependent on what the public relations professional believes the reporters will need. A typical media kit will contain the following information:

- Media release about the topic
- Detailed information on the product or service being discussed
- Detailed information about the structure and investments of the organization—main business activities, size, market position, revenues, products, key executives, and so on
- Maybe Frequently Asked Questions—or questions you wish the reporter would ask
- Biographies of key spokespeople
- Photo or video images. These are most typically given in digital format, either on CD or mini USB drive. To save a reporter's time, also print thumb size images, which the reporter can choose without having to look through the whole image bank.
- Media contact information

Most reporters in this region want to be handed a printed media release and kit on arrival, so they can refer to it during the presentations. This is especially necessary for financial data. Other reporters may, however, prefer to receive just a printed media release and be given the rest of the kit in digital format, or via hyperlinks in the media release document. A public relations professional will ensure that all options have been covered.

Case Study

Sony Australia launched *The Getaway*, PlayStation 2's most realistic driving action and adventure game in 2002. The company developed a media teaser campaign to build excitement around the Getaway-branded website. Media were to experience the realism and "virtual world" of the game. Sony used an East London gangster theme, core to the game, to create London screenscape postcards which were sent to journalists, with an opportunity to take a phone-call from "a friend of Charlie's"—a character in the game.

When it came to the launch, Sony thought big and employed a double-decker bus tour, with a cockney-rhyming slang pub quiz and actors role-playing to generate media coverage in men's titles like *FHM*.

Source: Asia Pacific PR Awards 2003.

Feature Articles

In addition to media releases, feature articles offer a good opportunity for generating coverage. These articles tend to be less focused on news, and more on the issues around the news. The most common way to place a feature article is to prepare an article and then contact the appropriate journalists to offer the story—either to use in whole or part, or as a basis for an interview or his own story.

Feature stories usually have one or more purposes:

- To inform
- To entertain
- To give practical guidance

It is, of course, harder to write a feature article than a news release. You need to capture the attention of the reader, and keep their attention throughout the feature. Feature articles vary in length—they may be as short as 400 words, or up to a 1,500 for an in-depth article. There are also no format rules for writing a feature article, but take a look at articles in any reputable publication and you will see that they tend to be written in the following style.

A. Headline   Similar to a news release, the headline should be sufficiently interesting to attract the reader. However, there is more license to be creative.

B. Lead   As in a media release, the lead needs to draw in the reader. Unlike a media release, you do not need to cover all the "whys and wheres" of the story—it can serve as a teaser. There are many different types of leads, but overall, they tend to fall into six categories:

1. *Summary*—simply telling the reader what the article is about.
2. *Narrative*—anecdotes, examples, or short histories, which set the scene and tone.
3. *Striking*—an unusual or controversial thought or statement.
4. *Quotations*—words enclosed in quotation marks or set off in some distinctive form such as a statement by someone, an excerpt from literature, or a letter.

5. *Question*—posed to the readers at the beginning to provoke interest, and ensure they are not content until they find out how the writer answers it.

6. *Direct*—a personal appeal. The writer is effectively talking to each reader individually instead of writing for everyone.

C. Body of Article   This section provides the substance of the story. It is generally written in order of importance of the information, or chronologically.

D. Conclusion   Unlike a media release, a feature article should include a summary of the key points at the end, or maybe a "call for action."

Op-Eds

A good way to gain credible visibility for an organization is for senior executives or experts to submit an op-ed to a major newspaper or magazine. Op-eds help an organization or individual gain high-quality coverage, reaching an elite audience of opinion-leaders.

The word "op-ed" originated from the tradition of newspapers placing readers' opinions on the page opposite their own editorial page. The word op-ed has, however, evolved into its own short form for the words "opinion editorial."

Whatever the terminology, an op-ed is a form of written opinion that addresses current issues or public policies. Approximately 700–800 words in length, it follows the same format as a feature article, but can be written in either the first or third person. The whole point of an op-ed is to state an opinion. This being the case, it is important to state your conclusion first, and then use the rest of the copy to support your conclusion.

Other factors to consider:

- Focus your writing tightly on one issue or idea
- Express your opinion—do not be equivocal
- Be timely, controversial, but also be a voice of reason
- Be personal and conversational; it can help you make your point
- Be humorous, if appropriate

Letters to the Editor and Response to Online Content

Letters to the editor or responses to online content offer an opportunity to either set the record straight or further expand a discussion topic.

In print form, letters to the editor usually respond or react to news stories, editorials, or other letters that appeared in a print publication in recent days or weeks. A letter might take issue with or agree with a reporter's description of the facts or with something said by a person quoted in an article. It is easy to dismiss this section as only read by retirees. However, they receive attention from political leaders, activists, and community residents, and are well worth the time and effort spent to have one published.

How to write the letter or response:

- The biggest challenge of letters is making a compelling point in a brief space while still ensuring that readers can follow your argument— even if they did not see the news story to which you're responding. The key to successful letters is brevity. Write an absolute maximum of 400 words—the ideal length is between 150 and 250 words. If your letter is too long, it either will not be published or cut short. Online responses can, of course, be longer as you will be able to post the whole message. However, again, keep it short, so readers need not scroll down the page and potentially lose interest.

- For a letter, be sure to include your full first and last name, address, phone and/or fax numbers (day and evening), and your e-mail address at the top of the letter. The editor is likely to need to check that you really exist before printing the letter.

- If referring to a previously published letter, a news story, or Internet item, identify it by its headline and the date it was published. This allows the editor to quickly check the original item to verify any references you have made to it.

- If appropriate, be witty but avoid worn-out clichés and weak puns.

- If you are responding negatively to a columnist's or blogger's views (or any other opinion piece), do not launch a personal attack on the writer, instead take issue with their views.

- Letters editors want to give as many people as possible a chance to comment on the issues, so be prepared for commentary on your own letter, in turn.

VNRs, ANRs, and B-Roll

Video News Releases (VNRs) are the electronic version of media releases and kits, which are sent to the broadcast media in the hope that they will feature them in a news program or magazine type program. (Note: the use of the word "video" is obsolete these days, given the digital formats in use these days. However, they continue to be referred to as video.) They provide prepackaged video footage and narration in the style of a television news story. An Audio News Release (ANRs) is the same, but for radio only. B-roll on the other hand, is loosely edited video footage a station uses to create its own story.

VNRs were not popular in Asia Pacific in the 1980s and 1990s, despite their prevalence in Europe and the United States. This was because there were not enough broadcast stations to justify the preparation expense. Similarly, the European and US model of working with VNR distribution companies was not effective because, again, with few stations it was more efficient for the public relations professional to contact them directly.

However, with the globalization of news, many companies are now providing footage on their own websites, and there are several companies, such as www.thenewsmarket.com, which provide web-based video, audio, and still marketing and distribution—in multiple Asian languages. Journalists simply register on the site and are notified when anything of interest is posted on the site, and download it directly for themselves.

Giving Good E-mail

E-mail is probably the most customary way we contact the media these days; even more so than by the telephone. This is why the "e-mail pitch" has become as important as a media release.

A good e-mail pitch will do the same job as a media release – attracting the journalist's attention at the beginning. Like a media release, we should look at the following elements:

1. Create a clear and attractive e-mail subject—which is interesting but not ambiguous

2. Create an enticing lead. (who, what, when, where, why, how?) Do not use *"I am writing to enquire whether you would be so kind as to cover this story..."* Instead, give a brief summary, a short anecdote, or a striking statement

3. Immediately after, tell the reporter why you are sending the e-mail. For example, you would like to invite the reporter to interview (spokesperson) who can talk about (topic)

4. The next one or two paragraphs should cover why the news is interesting, the story angles, or why the interviewee is worth talking to

5. Finish with any essential information. For example, if pitching an interview, give details of the where and when the interview will take place. Or if a feature, any supporting information you can provide (facts, figures, photos, video, and so on)

6. Conclude with your next steps and contact information. If culturally correct, do not ask the reporter to contact you, as they will contact you anyway if it is a good story. Instead, tell them when you will contact them again. Editors/reporters are blunt and will tell you when you call if they are interested or not

Three more tips for good media e-mail:

- Try to keep your e-mail to one screen of the computer, so the reporter does not have to scroll down to find any important information.

- Should you send attachments? Not so long ago, many editors and reporters were complaining about the size of e-mails being sent to them—they were so large that they crashed their systems. This was especially true of freelancers and foreign correspondents who worked from home. With the arrival of broadband, this has become less of a problem. It is still, however, worth considering if you need to send an attachment at all. If you do, a good guide is that if it takes more than five seconds to transmit from your computer to a colleague, then it is too large to send to send to a journalist.

- Be wary of different language software. Your Chinese or Korean characters may end up as gobbledygook in an e-mail, if they are not compatible.

The Best Time to Contact a Reporter

Finally, a chapter on the media would not be complete without addressing this question. Naturally, there is no hard and fast rule. However, in general, newspaper writers in Asia Pacific come to work at around 10 a.m. Major newspapers will hold their daily planning meeting between 10 a.m. and 11 a.m., when they decide which news they are going to follow up on, and if they will attend your media conference. Public relations professionals typically find it easiest to speak to a reporter between 11 a.m. and 2 p.m., before they leave the office to chase up news stories.

Deadlines for daily newspapers begin at around 5 p.m.; so there is little point in calling a reporter after 4 p.m., unless you have a genuine "hold the front page" story. The rule is a little different, however, for financial news, which can be released only after the stock markets close, in case the news has an impact on shares. In this situation, public relations professionals will notify the media in advance of the release time, and the editor will allocate space accordingly.

The old days are gone when you could count on your story being covered if you issued your news on a Sunday, when there are fewer reporters on call. Internet access and global news sources mean there is no shortage of news for the Monday edition. However, there will be little, if any, financial news being released on a Monday, which means there will be more space for "softer" stories. This is why we almost always see charity events or political rallies take place on a Sunday; it is not just because this is when people have free time.

Twenty-four-hour TV and radio news programs run all day, and the only time they may not accept your call is in the last 10 minutes before their hourly or regular show begins. Morning radio producers are gone by midday so, unless you enjoy early rising, they are best reached by e-mail.

CHAPTER 4

Public Relations and Branding: PR as a Complete Brand-Building Toolbox

I t's Friday and you plan to go out to the cinema. You reach for your local newspaper and scan the cinema listings. The latest blockbuster superhero movie, *Talisman*, catches your eye as the visuals in the small movie poster look intriguing. You haven't heard anything about it at all—so you turn back to the ad and take a closer look and start to read, "Prepare to enter another universe to do battle with the awesome power of Talisman! One man—one machine. An astonishing triumph of good over evil!" It sounds great—but the hyped language puts you off more than a little, so you turn to the movie column where you read a pithy piece about the movie by the local film critic, "Superhero schlock can be fun as long as it is action packed, right-on, and has the wow factor impact. *Talisman* lacks it all—it is just plain clunky. And it rings as hollow as that iron suit. A franchise has come to life, but we're still looking around for its superhero to make an appearance." And so your mind is made up—you go back to the movie list and start to look for another film.

The scenario outlined above is one that we surely all recognize. In our busy lives, a decision such as this, while clearly not a matter of life or death, is still an important consumer choice, made alongside the thousands of others we make during our brief or enduring relationships with products and services. Whether choosing movies to watch, clothes to wear, universities to attend, airlines to fly with, or banks to trust, millions of people throughout Asia Pacific are entering into a relationship with a supplier that confirms their right to make informed decisions in the marketplace for shampoo, hedge funds, or travel destinations.

But the most pertinent aspect of this scenario is in demonstrating that most people base their purchase decisions on the recommendations of credible third-party endorsers, rather than on the subjective corporate pitch from the industry actually producing the product or service. Often, this form of puffery is viewed with real suspicion by consumers. Aside from being overblown, it is also overused and most audiences screen it out as a consequence and seek out more credible information sources.

Public Relations and Marketing Battle It Out

"While advertising is what you pay for, public relations is what you pray for."[1]

Philip Kotler, marketing guru

Public relations and marketing are distinct professional entities. They use different language to refer to their end users. Marketing and advertising professionals speak of target markets, consumers, and customers, while public relations professionals refer to publics, audiences, and stakeholders. Yet, their worlds overlap under the banner of marketing communications. Their function and purpose is similar, as both are concerned with enhancing end user relationships and both firmly believe in mobilizing communication to get the best message out about their products and services in order to increase sales.

Marketing involves pinpointing and meeting consumer needs often for profit. PR, on the other hand, is concerned with using planned communication to build good stakeholder relationships and create positive predispositions toward an organization and its products and services.

In essence, they are both aiming to achieve the same end, and although they are taking a different route to do so, they both need each other. PR is a recognized part of the marketing strategic mix and resides alongside advertising, direct marketing, and sponsorship as ways of promoting the brand and as a consequence, it is integral to the marketing communications effort. So, PR is recognized by the marketing world as a critical part of the integrated marketing communications (IMC) arsenal.

But PR is increasingly seen to be taking one of the more important roles within the IMC process. And because of this new development, other components of IMC, such as advertising, are sitting up and taking notice.

"Advertising and promotion are about salesmanship. PR is about information. Consumers know it and are on the defensive about being sold something they don't want or need. By providing information to consumers directly or through trusted third parties, PR makes advertising more believable, and promotion more actionable. That is why it [public relations] is the secret weapon of integrated marketing. Public relations is uniquely able to close the marketing credibility gap."[2]

Thomas L. Harris, marketing public relations expert

Many practitioners now regard PR as a critical way of winning over the hearts and minds of consumers by creating a favorable shift in attitudes and behavior to boost the turnover of products and services. PR can help develop new markets, promote new products, position and reposition organizations and their output in new, existing, and future markets. Applying strategic communications campaigns, including the all important third-party endorsements by opinion makers and influentials, a corporate image or product can be strengthened, sustained, and safeguarded for as long as the PR effort continues. Underpinning this effort is the ultimate ability of PR to forge lasting links between brands and customers—a meaningful union that should hopefully last forever.

Case Study

In a creative and farsighted community-based campaign, oil company Castrol India worked with rural communities beset by drought to solve the problem of water shortages. The intention here was also to establish engagement with these communities and to generate more brand recognition locally for Castrol CRB-Plus oil, utilized by local farmers as tractor fuel. The overall objective was to implement a water management system that could be sustained and duplicated, bringing together input from the local rural community, NGOs, and government bodies.

To ensure a long-standing solution to the serious local drought issue, research was undertaken in these geographic areas resulting in workable, successful schemes such as water harvesting, based on an irrigation strategy and a watershed initiative. Other solutions were provided in consultation with local NGOs taking the form of canal rehabilitation, monitoring, and development.

A localized, below-the-line and media relations approach was taken, including local dialect-based traditional performances, launch events of dam construction projects, and "tractor meets" which enabled Castrol to publicize their involvement.

The success of this venture was measured by the successful recall for CRB-Plus oil that increased from 45 percent to 91 percent resulting from this campaign.

Source: Asia Pacific PR Awards 2003.

All About the Brand

"PR creates the brand ... You can launch a new brand only with public relations."
   Al Ries & Laura Ries, The Fall of Advertising and the Rise of PR

Public relations is now getting the credit for successful brand building and for breathing life into the brand, and it's none too early. This evolution of PR's branding role is recognized as a sort of coming-of-age for the industry and a wider indication of the relevance of relationship building between an organization and key audiences based on credible communication.

The received wisdom from today's marketers is that brands are built over time and not overnight. In this sense, strategic PR campaigns enable an organization such as Starbucks or H&M to create the marketing buzz and word-of-mouth support by projecting the brand profile through a range of communications activities to get the targeted message out, including special events and targeted editorial coverage. This approach not only positions the brand by capturing consumer attention, but also enables the brand relationship to be developed and sustained over time.

Case Study

The first restaurant in Australia licensed to cater for dogs and their owners, "My Dog Café," was launched in Melbourne in March 2006.

The "My Dog Café" campaign by the Graffiti Group was launched to reach core consumers and attract new loyalists to drive sales growth for the restaurant. The objective of the media relations campaign and "red carpet" launch event was to build a robust, emotional brand connection and develop brand loyalty for the canine eatery, in addition to launching its latest product, Finest Cuts, a gourmet dog food range.

MasterFoods and leading chef Andrew Blake partnered up and masterminded the initiative, "My Dog Café," creating an emotional, unique eating experience. The café offered the ultimate culinary destination for dog lovers and their four-legged friends. The idea of a specialist café serving tasty morsels for dogs and their owners generated a wide amount of media interest and resulting coverage, which brought many new customers to the dog café.

Source: Asia Pacific PR Awards 2006.

Locating the brand—what is it?

- Why would people buy Vegemite instead of Marmite in Australia?
- Why is Cathay Pacific Hong Kong's favorite airline?
- Why do all age groups across Asia reach for Tiger Balm ointment when they have a headache or muscle sprain?
- Why do you buy your regular brand of toothpaste or shampoo, rather than the no label version, other than to save money?
- The perennial—Coca-Cola or Pepsi?

The answer is that a brand in the heart and mind of the consumer equates to an assured guarantee of quality, status, and desired lifestyle. Or let's put the question another way—what brand comes to mind when you need toilet tissue or sticky tape, a cup of coffee, a hotel room, or bottled water?

Point of View

"There are so many brands now in China that it is important to build up a strong relationship with your consumer and through any contact point that will build their relationship. Previously, it used to be the mass media but we are now looking at contact points. They could be anything that consumers come into contact with. For example, it could be point of sales, events, TV program sponsorship, or event sponsorship. You will find that even for a handphone, consumers can name up to 36 contact points they come across and that is huge. You have to find out which are the contact points that stand out."[3]

Linda Tan, General Manager, Zenith Media, Beijing, *Branding in China* (2005)

More than a name

A brand is so much more than a product name, a differentiating corporate logo and trademark, memorable tagline, or repetitive jingle. The message-weary, sophisticated consumer tunes out all of these superficial aspects of brand architecture if that's all that exists of the brand itself.

The relationship between the brand and its consumers is paramount as has always been the case and the glue that binds this together is trust. Time-challenged consumers and customers want to invest time and money in products, services, businesses, and people that they can rely on to deliver the brand promise.

The intangible aspects of the branded product or service appear to be the most significant factors in the branding process. These are centered on a collection of consumer feelings, attitudes, and beliefs about the uniqueness of the brand. They aim to fulfill needs and desires through highlighting the brand's core features and benefits—both real and imagined on both a rational and emotional basis. They also enable the brand to be instantly recognizable and much desired. Invariably, it is the emotional attachments of the consumer to the brand in terms of its recognizable identity or personality that is the most compelling in developing the all-powerful mindshare.

This goes a long way to ensuring that the brand is recognizable and has its competitive edge in place. Once this brand identity is established, the competitive advantage is secure, it can't be stolen or replicated by a competitor, and longevity of the brand is now a very strong possibility.

But branding does not just simply happen—and if it did, then it would be out of control and out of focus. That is where public relations comes into its own in the branding process by using a credible communication strategy to elevate and support the value and power of the brand among audiences. Taking this approach, both the external and internal communications strategy as part of the brand strategy blueprint will enhance awareness, comprehension, and commitment to the brand among key stakeholders who impact the organization's business outcomes.

Case Study

When TMP Worldwide changed its name to Hudson, the challenge was to motivate employees to embrace a new vision and values.

Impact Communications Australia achieved this by designing a "Blueprint" planning workshop to understand employee sentiment. An inspirational video was created, and a fully integrated road show for employees rolled out across all major cities in Australia and New Zealand.

Results were extremely positive, with over 96 percent of employees saying they felt proud to work at Hudson.

Source: Asia Pacific PR Awards 2004.

A Holistic Public Relations Approach

Successful and sustainable branding is predicated on ensuring that the whole organizational output, from internal staff communication and behavior to external activities and the physical environment, are all encompassed under the same brand umbrella or parasol—come rain or shine. The branding opportunity for an organization using PR to drive this forward is realized in anchoring the organization's vision and mission, its operations, behaviors, and activities at all levels across the organizational strata. All internal and external communication about the brand must be sung from the same page of the song sheet and should tell the same story.

Brand identity is the most essential aspect of the brand and must be built from the inside out—to nurture the soul of the organization. Next, the brand must be reinforced with an outside-in approach that expresses the essence of the brand to differentiate it from the crowd—placing it in pole position in stakeholders' minds.

PR's role in all of this is to ensure that brand identity—its personality and image—are perfectly aligned, thereby closing the perception gap in the mind of the stakeholder. The brand image based on the customer experience and the communications package (voice, tone, content, scope) should deeply reflect the overall brand identity. Renovating a high-rise building and spending the majority of the budget on the lobby and entrance hall—so often seen in Asian collectivist cultures where "face" is the most valued aspect of the deal—will not build or sustain the brand or assure any type of brand equity across time.

Equally, we can't claim that our hotel offers a top-class guest experience if the front desk employees are rude, or are unable to answer basic questions from occupants, or if the rooms are not cleaned to the anticipated professional standards. The value of the brand is based on performing well and getting due credit for that. But this can't be founded on empty taglines and hollow promotional promises in corporate websites and promotional leaflets or in CEO media interviews. It is also about establishing interconnectivity through employee training programs and robust recognition and reward schemes that encourage employees to recognize and execute brand-based values and behaviors in their performance, which will result in high levels of customer satisfaction and an assured corporate reputation.

At the end of the day, we can't claim a country to be a desirable and world-class tourist destination if the daily pollution levels are so high that they not only obscure the local views, but also pose a real health hazard.

Brand warning: Don't promise to deliver when you know you cannot.

Point of View

"Brand building in China requires more harmony with the regional governments than in most countries. Governments recognize good corporate citizenship helps brands not only reach Chinese consumers' minds but also their hearts."

David Zhao, General Manager, Hill & Knowlton Shanghai

Public Relations and Branding—the Ten Unavoidable Laws

1. *Be sensitive to the local but don't neglect the global*

   Brands should engender global respect, trust, and reach but be sensitive to the localities of Asia Pacific and their indigenous cultures. Public relations efforts can ensure that the brand is credible in all markets by being local and acting global. Most successful global brands started from a strong home base and expanded regionally or internationally on the back of a well-established brand image.

2. *It's all about the relationships*

   Brands are customer-driven in a consumer economy—as the intention is to reach the right consumers, at the right time, in the right way to create a lifelong relationship. Good research will be critical in trying to reach Asia Pacific consumers and to connect with them. We need to get inside their heads and hearts, if they are to relate to the brand ethos as they would their best friend.

3. *Position and understand the brand internally and externally*

   Before thinking of promoting the brand ensure that its ethos, identity, and positioning are well in place so that it can take on the marketplace and the competition and prove its differentiators effortlessly. Avoid being misrepresented by stakeholders, including employees—get the brand message out loud and clear to the customer.

4. *The brand is all (just don't tell everyone)*

   Everything is branded these days and it's all about the brand and developing those positive emotional and rational connections between the all-powerful customer and the brand. Public relations activities—from publicity to promotions—are well suited to developing these perception-based links.

5. *Be in it for the long-term*

   Building up a brand takes patience and time, particularly in the more conservative cultures of Asia Pacific. Brands are built-up over time and not overnight. Public relations operates well within this agenda. The PR approach can use a variety of short- and long-term, cost-effective and creative communication strategies to introduce and sustain the brand in the marketplace. In this way, customer

(Continued)

understanding and brand devotion can be strategically developed with lasting results.

6. *Identify and nurture brand allies*

   Brand communications is all about making the right connections with the right stakeholders. This is the what PR does well if not best—forming strategic alliances, which in building and nurturing brands is essential to establishing and keeping their market share.

7. *Media Matters*

   Third-party endorsement is critical to brand development so public relations can do what it does well and use editorials in traditional media channels to deliver the brand message in an independent and credible manner. It can also boost the brand via grassroots, word-of-mouth, consumer-to-consumer, and one-to-one style endorsements in blogs and social networking sites.

8. **Communicate brand values consistently**

   The brand message must be consistent and true to the core brand values as this underpins the trust that builds and sustains the customer's brand loyalty. This resides at the core of the PR strategic approach where consistent messages across all communication channels are always the rule of thumb.

9. **For better or for worse keep investing in the brand**

   Even in the worst of times, it pays to keep investing in and promoting the brand because the loyalty has to be maintained and the markets will rebound eventually. PR comes into its own in harsh economic environments as it can use low cost options to boost brand profiles in creative ways using viral or guerilla style marketing communications approaches or integrated brand messaging through targeted messaging via digital channels.

10. *Bin the spin and be true to the brand*

    PR can go beyond the spin—not that it was ever there—to develop the believability factor and build a sustainable brand reputation to develop brand credibility and loyalty based on consumer relevance. PR will soon be recognized as the premier brand-building practice in the business of protecting and promoting the brand promise.

Case Study

The humble kiwifruit—arguably New Zealand's most iconic product—has been the source of considerable creativity and collaboration throughout Asia Pacific by GolinHarris, which works with the world's premier kiwifruit brand, ZESPRI. Each year, the objectives are to boost ZESPRI kiwifruit sales, media coverage, and brand recognition by promoting the fruit's quality, taste, and nutritional benefits.

GolinHarris adopts an approach tailored to different audiences across each market. In the past several years, GolinHarris has implemented the following programs:

Beijing: A family dinnertime campaign was developed in response to the fact that while this had traditionally played an important role in Chinese family life, dinner was being sacrificed as people worked longer and resorted to dining out. GolinHarris developed this into a national family campaign, communicating the nutritional and familial values of sharing kiwifruit at home. After conducting an online survey, GolinHarris held a media conference to promote the "2030" concept: going home before 20:30 and devoting 20-30 minutes daily to enjoy fruit and family time, drawing scores of media hits in Beijing, Shanghai, and Guangzhou.

Shanghai: GolinHarris worked with ZESPRI to exceed sales goals by 360 percent—despite the brand's premium product status and comparatively high price—through two campaigns. GolinHarris screened a video inside an aircraft cabin—a notoriously poor environment for skin—while a nutritionist endorsed kiwifruit as a source of nutrients for the skin and also as a way to prevent deep vein thrombosis. The team also partnered with a women's website to hold a "kiwi wedding" for newlyweds to profess their "kiwi love," spreading the message that health is the best gift for your partner.

Hong Kong: ZESPRI and GolinHarris conducted a nutritional study with Hong Kong University, researching the effects of kiwifruit on constipation. The findings were the subject of a major media relations campaign further underpinning the health benefits of kiwifruit consumption. Also, the team partnered with a local restaurant chain to promote the inclusion of ZESPRI kiwifruit in school lunches. In one day, ZESPRI gave away 45,000 pieces of kiwifruit at 70 schools. The campaign finished with thousands of children, parents, and teachers joining together at a local stadium to enjoy kiwifruit—and a choir of 1,000 children singing an original song about kiwifruit.

(Continued)

Taiwan: GolinHarris researched the benefits of consuming kiwifruit before going to sleep at night. The positive results were announced at an
innovative press conference that featured a kiwifruit bed designed to look
like an actual kiwifruit farm.

Singapore: GolinHarris helped its audience "get in bed" with ZESPRI as it
leveraged the research results from Taiwan into a new campaign. Focusing
on the message that eating two kiwifruit one hour before bedtime improves
sleep, GH organized a pajama party in Singapore's New Majestic Hotel.

GolinHarris has helped ZESPRI generate hundreds of media clippings,
millions of dollars in equivalent advertising value, and triple-digit increases in kiwifruit sales over the past six years across these key markets.

Source: GolinHarris Hong Kong.

Branding the Bottom Line

Managing and communicating brands effectively can directly impact the
bottom line of an organization's livelihood by raising the levels of performance and assuring external credibility. Not only that, when global economies enter recessionary waters, the marketing budget is often the first thing
to be grounded on dry land. As public relations is the lower cost route compared with other more expensive options in the marketing communications
stable such as advertising, it also becomes a more attractive choice for brand
building in a global economic downturn—and it stands the test of time. But
PR must still ensure that any impact it has on establishing the brand identity
and maintaining the brand equity of an organization and its deliverables is
easily measurable in real terms.

Endnotes

1. Kotler, P., *Kotler on Marketing* (New York: The Free Press, 1999), 111.
2. Harris, T.L., *Value-Added Public Relations* (Lincolnwood, IL: NTC Business
   Books, 1998), 10.
3. *Branding in China: The Media Platforms Reaching 1.3 Billion Consumers* (Singapore:
   China Knowledge Press, 2005).

CHAPTER 5

Building and Defending Corporate Reputation

A great deal has been written on the topic of corporate reputation, also called corporate image and corporate brand. It's not surprising, as corporate communications is the foundation of all public relations. Before we have a product, we have a company who makes the product. The reputation of that company with its stakeholders will help set it apart from the competition, who may be offering similar products and services. In this sense, the corporate reputation should be geared toward helping stakeholders to engage positively with the organization as consumers, employees, shareholders, or sponsors, for example.

A good corporate reputation effectively provides companies with a "social license" to operate.

There are big payoffs in developing a good corporate reputation:

1. Increased customer preference
2. Ability to charge a premium for products and services
3. Superior financial performance
4. Ability to attract and retain high caliber employees
5. Greater external support and solidarity in times of crisis

Corporate reputation is an increasingly critical concern for CEOs globally. A 2003 survey of C-suite executives in Asia, North America, and Europe—Corporate Reputation Watch—by Hill & Knowlton and Korn/Ferry International, found that Asian-based executives were actually more focused on utilizing corporate reputation to achieve business results than their North American and European counterparts.

The Harris-Fombrun Reputation Quotient also gives us a useful way to look at the factors that make up a corporate reputation. The model was developed by global market research and polling firm Harris Interactive and Dr. Charles Fombrun of The Reputation Institute (www.harrisinteractive.com).

It tells us that there are six key drivers of corporate reputation:

1. Emotional Appeal: how people feel about a company; whether they admire and trust the company

2. Products and Services: the quality, value, innovation, and customer service behind products and services

3. Vision and Leadership: the skill and vision of the CEO and leadership team

4. Workplace Engagement: how well it is managed, and whether it attracts good employees

5. Financial Performance: the track record of profitability, growth prospects, and competitive place

6. Social responsibility: the level of a company's environmental and social responsibility, and its human rights track record

Communications clearly has a major role to play in imparting knowledge about the above drivers. However, communication has to be based on reality and on real organizational behavior. The company clearly has to walk the talk. No amount of image packaging will create a positive reputation for a company performing poorly in the financial, operational, and corporate responsibility area.

Developing a Corporate Reputation Program

A corporate communications program aims to identify how a company or organization is currently perceived by its audiences, and determine and implement a strategy that improves or even changes those perceptions.

Point of View

"Corporate realities are what we need to communicate in corporate communications. Only corporate realities provide substance. Suppose we are asked to communicate on a topic which does not actually exist—what do we do? We cannot say the company is something that it is not.

What we can do is to help create that reality. This is where alignment of behavior and goals, through disciplined internal communications, take place. And while we are at it, we might as well go an extra distance to help turn a good company into a great organization."

Shuri Fukunaga, Managing Director, Market Leader Burson-Marsteller Tokyo

---

A successful corporate communications program can achieve the following benefits:

1. Establishes a clear and concise definition around the organization brand and everything it stands for

2. Communicates powerful messaging and proof points that resonate with stakeholders

3. Creates a meaningful experience and differentiation with stakeholders

4. Makes an internal commitment to the company mission, vision, and values

5. Enables consistent global communications

Driving reputation

To implement a successful corporate communications program, first we need to understand the business goals, and determine what barriers are standing in the way of achieving them, and what are the drivers that will help us on our way. Barriers could include a lack of differentiation from the competition, or a simple lack of understanding by a key audience. Drivers could be having a popular flagship product or a strong ethical policy.

By looking at the barriers and drivers, we can decide how we go about reaching these goals and how we can align them with organizational strategic objectives as a whole for sustained impact. But corporate identity management should most usefully be aligned with stakeholder expectations.

Case Study

The paper industry sometimes comes under criticism for its perceived poor environmental and human rights issues. Thailand's SCG Paper and Ogilvy PR Worldwide launched "The Inspiration on Paper" campaign in 2008 to tell consumers about the benefit of buying paper from environmentally-friendly producers, like SCG Paper. This saw the creation of "Paper Town," a consumer event that demonstrated the role of creativity and innovation in SCG's mission to develop environment-friendly processes and products.

The company's guide to calculating consumers' carbon footprints and a fashion show featuring evening gowns and dresses made of recycled paper were well received by the audience. A media briefing and media trips to the company's tree plantations and manufacturing facilities in Thailand and the Philippines rounded off the campaign.

Source: Asia Pacific PR Awards 2008.

So, who are the people who really count and who can influence our reputation? And what can we do to reinforce or alter their mindset to our benefit? What can we control practically to effect a change in reputation?

Similar to branding, the findings are honed to denote the company's differentiation and messages. From here, it is relatively simple to move to strategy development and the actual corporate reputation program.

Typical elements of a corporate communications program will be based on a "thought leadership" structure, designed to show that the corporation is a leader in its field, one to be trusted for advice and opinions.

Thought leadership can be conveyed in various ways:

- Research—into the thought leadership topic; demonstrating the company's viewpoint or leadership in the area.
- Media relations—meetings, interviews, and media releases which discuss current topics and issues
- Speaking opportunities
- White papers—a case for the company's vision
- By-lined articles—confirming the viewpoint of the company, written by senior executives

- Op-eds—opinionated by-lined articles
- Case studies—demonstrating how the company has addressed the thought leadership issue
- Digital—messages on the company website
- Community activity—including advisory panels and community site speeches
- Stakeholder activity—meetings, seminars, and networking at events
- Internal—intranet, newsletters, town hall meetings

Corporate identity is a separate topic from corporate image or corporate reputation, and difficult to define. In essence, it captures the desired "persona" or symbol of an organization. It allows customers, suppliers, and staff to instantly recognize an organization, and usually makes itself felt through verbal branding such as the company name and visual branding, such as logos, advertising, brochures, building signs, websites, signs on transport, employee uniforms, and stationery.

Global companies, such as McDonald's and Google, and Japan's Toyota and Honda, are instantly recognizable though the Golden Arches, the double "oo" and festive "oogles," and distinctive car emblems.

CEOs in the Spotlight

It is accepted lore now that CEOs and company reputation are deeply and inextricably linked.

CEO successes, departures, and failures make headlines around Asia and the world. With the spotlight on CEOs, leaders need to understand and leverage the close link between their reputations and that of the company. A well-thought-of CEO can produce many happy returns, starting with the bottom line. This is particularly true across Asia where respect for authority is embedded into the value systems of most organizations. Employees can invest considerable emotion into being associated with their CEO, which brings an additional expectation to CEO behavior.

Although we may well know rationally that the CEO is not the company; on an emotional level, the CEO is perceived as the embodiment of the company's heart and mind.

CEOs set the tone, define company direction, attract talent, and are the human face of the organization. However, it raises the question whether a company's reputation may flow from the personality of its CEO, or whether the CEO has to be shaped and molded to fit the company? Are they really themselves, or just under the strict orders of a team of advisors and brand managers?

Corporate scandals such as those of Lehman Brothers, AIG, Enron, and WorldCom have raised the bar as far as protecting a corporation's reputation is concerned. Warren Buffett, the renowned US investor, businessman, and philanthropist, said it for us all: "It takes 20 years for us to build a reputation and five minutes to lose it. If you think about that, you will do things differently."[1]

In today's business environment, top executives must be able to represent and lead their corporate brand. Leaders of world-class Asian companies like Lenovo's Chairman Yang Yuanqing; Satoru Iwata, CEO of Nintendo, and N.R. Narayana Murthy, Chairman of the Board and Chief Mentor of Infosys Technologies are all directly involved in leading their corporate visions and strategies. Their visibility supports their company business results.

Just a few years ago, it was apparent that many CEOs rose to their positions of authority because they were particularly good at their job and not because they knew how to communicate effectively. No longer. Communications has become a primary part of the balanced score card. It would be rare to find a CEO or a multinational corporate who does not have some flair and understanding of the importance of communications.

Research into CEO behavior by public relations consultancies has been a popular thought leadership activity in recent years. First off the block was Burson-Marsteller, whose 2005 Building CEO Capital™ study indicated that the CEO's reputation is responsible for nearly 50 percent of a company's reputation, directly translating into achieving key business objectives and increasing sales.

The survey showed clearly the payoffs of a strong CEO reputation, including:

- 95 percent of people would consider the CEO when deciding whether to invest in a company.
- 94 percent would believe in a company under pressure from the media if they approved of the CEO.

- 93 percent would recommend a company as a good alliance/merger partner partly based on the reputation of the CEO.
- 92 percent would still have confidence in a company when the share price lags if they also have confidence in the CEO.
- 88 percent would recommend the company as a good place to work if they felt positively about the CEO.

The fly in the ointment, however, was highlighted in the 2007 Safeguarding Reputation™ survey by Weber Shandwick and KRC Research, which found that global business executives assign nearly 60 percent of the blame to CEOs when companies lose reputation in the aftermath of a crisis. According to this survey, the researchers did not find any significant differences between Asia, Europe, and North America.

CEO reputation programs can improve the visibility and stature of a CEO which, in turn, help a company differentiate its message and reputation; support its relationships with key customers, regulators, analysts, and other stakeholders; attract skilled staff; and have greater influence on the industry and regulatory agenda.

A 2007 PRWeek/Burson-Marsteller CEO survey polled 144 CEOs in the US about a variety of issues and found that 85.4 percent of CEOs believe it is "extremely important" or "important" to be perceived as an influencer in their industry.

This is why a key part of a corporate communications program is devoted to raising the profile of the CEO. The main activities of a CEO program would be similar to that of the overall corporate communications

---

Point of View

"One of the fundamental changes I have seen in the PR industry in the past few years is that we no longer lament not having a seat at the board table. Blogs and the Internet equal faster, accurate and sometimes inaccurate, information flows which need to be managed. This has resulted in many CEOs we work with taking the proactive management of the public image of their company, products and services much more seriously, giving us as important a voice as finance, compliance and legal."

Emma Smith, CEO, The Consultancy Limited.

program but, of course, focused on the CEO. Media interaction for the CEO, speaking opportunities, articles, education pieces, and face-to-face meetings with regulators, government officers, are examples.

At the end of the day, corporate reputation can only be based on demonstrable reality. It must encapsulate the realities of the stakeholders and the organization's overall goals and activities. Style will never be a substitute for substance—it is not a "wrapper" around an organization; however attractive.

Corporate reputations are serious business. They produce substantial payoffs for a company in terms of financial performance and consumer support. Companies that consistently manage their reputations are undoubtedly the ones that will endure.

Ultimately, if organizations do not manage their own reputations, their publics will manage it for them.

Case Study

While corporate communication programs look to the long-term, there will be landmark events along the way, and National Association of Securities Dealers Automated Quotations (NASDAQ) employed such an event to raise its corporate profile.

Historically, NASDAQ has been the exchange of choice for many of China's most prominent, innovative companies listing in the United States. But in 2007, the competition had become increasingly fierce, as the New York Stock Exchange (NYSE) and numerous other foreign capital markets were vying for these listings. In mid-2007, NASDAQ asked Ogilvy PR/Beijing to help create an event that reaffirmed their commitment to China and reaffirmed their position as the exchange of choice for Chinese companies seeking to list on international capital markets.

NASDAQ needed an event that clearly differentiated the exchange in China. Borrowing from its famous "bell ringing" activity that symbolizes the opening of the market each day, NASDAQ decided to hold an unprecedented remote bell-ringing event in Beijing, China. The remote bell ringing ceremony was to be the high-profile event that would herald in a new era for NASDAQ in China.

The remote bell ringing ceremony was held in Beijing on the evening of April 3, 2007, and thus opened morning trading in the US. The event comprised of cocktail reception followed by a dinner for NASDAQ representatives, government officials, listed companies, and representatives

(Continued)

from companies that were considering listing. Then, guests joined media for the climax of the night—the countdown to the ringing of the bell.

More than 20 CEOs and CFOs from NASDAQ-listed Chinese companies joined the US Ambassador to China and Bob Greifeld, CEO of NASDAQ, on the stage to ring the bell. This image was picked-up by television stations across the world, with the signatures of the representatives on a specially designed podium displayed live on the 17 meter-high NASDAQ screen in the center of Times Square, New York City.

The NASDAQ remote bell ringing ceremony gained extensive coverage worldwide and demonstrated NASDAQ's strong commitment to China. Over one hour of news coverage was broadcast by 43 domestic Chinese media groups, and more than 35 articles were written about the event in domestic media including a front-page feature story published in China's largest English language publication, *China Daily*. The event was broadcast live on CNBC, Bloomberg TV, and CCTV, and video footage was replayed throughout the following day in reports about the NASDAQ-China relationship on both BBC World Asia and CNN Asia. It is, to date, the most prominent event that an international stock market has ever held in China. After the remote bell ringing ceremony, there was a sharp increase in the number of Chinese companies listing on NASDAQ. There were six new listings in the three months after the event, which made a total of 12 NASDAQ listings in the first half of 2007—a marked increase compared to the nine listings for all of 2006.

Source: Ogilvy PR Worldwide China.

Endnote

1. Buffet, M. and D. Clark, *The Tao of Warren Buffett* (New York: Scribner, 2006).

6

Marketing to Asia Pacific Consumers and Businesses

All marketing efforts begin and end with the customer. They are the start point for the manufacturer and service provider in the sense that goods and services are created for their identified needs and requirements. The push to produce those goods must be matched by the pull from the consumer to buy them in order to stimulate efficient economic exchange to survive and prosper in the business world.

The marketing chain from production of goods to distribution and supply though to the point-of-sale has to be managed not only tactically, by physically and logistically making it happen, but also more strategically by understanding the inner workings of the customers' mindset and their attitudes and feelings toward the producer and its products. This knowledge will develop a closer link with the customer to inform each side about the other in the process of adding value to the product and adding kudos to the organization.

Estranged Bedfellows

There appears to be a contested or uneven relationship between the realms of marketing and public relations founded on a matter of perspective. Marketers view public relations as a means to an end, or as an add-on promotional tool to assist the marketing drive, which is often reinforced by the ways that organizations have traditionally tended to downgrade or downscale the importance of communication in the overall management process. Significantly, this perception is changing as the value of communicating both wisely and well is increasingly being recognized as critical for all.

Meanwhile, in the opposite corner of the ring, public relations professionals see public relations as a vital management process and a set of synergistic communications activities that many of their stakeholders are actively engaged in—not just as purchasers of products and services, but also those who are involved in communicating with other businesses and forming business-to-business deals and partnerships. They would go so far as to claim that everyone needs to engage in public relations activities on a variety of levels and that everyone is doing public relations activities—in a small-, medium-, and large-scale way.

> "Megamarketing: involves the normal tools of marketing (the four Ps) plus two others: power and public relations... public relations is a pull strategy. Public opinion takes longer to cultivate, but when energized, it can pull the company into the market."[1]
>
> *Philip Kotler*

But not every organization in the Asia Pacific region is engaging in marketing or "megamarketing" activities in the strict sense of the term. The police force, for example, in Singapore, Australia, and Hong Kong are committed to interacting with stakeholders in the community and use media relations to inform those stakeholders about their local commitments. But, they don't encourage people to commit more crimes to keep the police in the job! While public relations professionals would acknowledge that marketing communications is part and parcel of the public relations portfolio— it is not the only focus of their work and it takes its place alongside issues management, media relations, public affairs, crisis communications, internal communications, and corporate communications in terms of a host of evolving communication based services that can be offered to organizations under the banner of reputation and management and acknowledgement for achievement. This is predicated on an understanding of the local community's belief and value systems and their prevailing attitudes and perceptions. In response to this knowledge, stakeholders can be incorporated into the business of building corporate reputations and supporting business goals. If they are for you, then they are not against you.

The role of public relations in the sphere of consumer relations is usually tagged as marketing communications or marcoms, which involves a range of activities from the communication portfolio often referred to as the promotional mix—including activities such as promotions, events, sponsorship, and advertising.

Point of View

"For almost every industry, Asia will be a key driver of growth for the next several decades. But this is also a vast and diverse continent where over two-thirds of the world's population speaks more than 2,000 languages. As Asian consumers get increasingly plugged in to the media mix—both traditional and online—PR is emerging as a vital tool for building relationships with our markets in places like India and China and laying the groundwork for a further push into these engines of 21st century businesses."

Sabrina Cheung, Director, Corporate Communications, adidas Asia Pacific

---

Mind Your Ps

Public relations is seen as a critical part of the promotional aspect of the marketing mix residing alongside other factors—the product, price, and place—which all have to be carefully managed in getting products to consumers for profitable gain. Traditionally, this marketing mix as part of the overall marketing effort encompasses the brand or product on offer, the asking price in the market, the place geographically and physically where it can be accessed, and promotion using media channels and informative yet enticing messages to persuade the consumer to buy the brand. Public relations is naturally located in the latter zone as it is in the business of facilitating relationships between an organization and its stakeholders—in this case, the buyers of products and services.

Yet, in reality the public relations approach should be involved across all of the Ps in the marketing mix and may well be integrated into the key messages being communicated to the customer. Price, for example, could be angled as a key promotional message in terms of its association with value for money or prestige—which for the Asian consumer of prestige goods is often a positive trigger. Or the place of distribution for the product may be a promotional feature as a new brand may enter the market accompanied by a flagship store as is often the case with global fashion brands in Asia—Armani and H&M launched their brands in Shanghai and Hong Kong by opening large retail outlets in commanding positions across these cities—which is very media-worthy both visually and story-wise.

This is where public relations professionals come into their own. You can't hope to sell something that no one has ever heard of. Someone has to get the message out to the customer about the efficacy of the product or service that will solve their problems and fulfill their desires in a more compelling way than the competitor, while at the same time monitoring consumers' shifting perceptions toward the brand over time and relaying this back to the organization responsible for production. Someone also has to be responsible for ensuring that this customer-product relationship stays sweet and acquires longevity. This requires constant communications upkeep in the form of on-going updates, reminders, prods, and invitations to buy and use the product or service or revisit the issue because it is the only solution to their problem, the only satisfaction for their need, the only product or service of its kind that has something big and life-changing in it for them that will align with their aspirations, and fulfill big promises in terms of their hopes and dreams. And all because it is a "Yes it will" sort of product or service.

But as we are aware, people do not buy products as such. They buy satisfactions of their wants and needs in terms of the benefits that products and services are supplying. In essence the PR message must always answer the customer's most pertinent question, "what is in this deal for me?"

This simple and direct question operates on two levels—the message must be so engagingly crafted in terms of the visual and verbal content at first glance and so attention-getting that the recipient stops, looks, and listens to it as they realize that there might well be something in it for them. Next, on closer inspection, having expended time and energy in understanding the message content, they should be convinced by the key messages in the advertorial, news article, blog, website, poster, or leaflet that this product or service is the only one for them. For this reason, in communicating the marcoms message across a range of media and formats, it is vital for the public relations practitioner to look beyond the product or service itself to the underlying motives of the people who want to buy it so that the marcoms message can be framed according to their world view and actual requirements giving it true resonance.

The Customer's Marcoms Mantra

- Don't sell them a mobile phone. Sell them connectivity. Innovation. Reliability. A cool design.
- Don't sell them a fashion brand. Sell them style. Attractiveness. Stunning appearance. A complete look.
- Don't sell them furniture. Sell them comfort. A new-look apartment. Design. Functionality.
- Don't sell them insurance. Sell them security. Opportunity. Reassurance. A real future.

Of course, the dialogue with the consumer must be as all-embracing as possible and consistency is the key here as the complete product offering must communicate the appeal on every level, from abstract promises and claims in the promotional materials and the actual brand name, to the physical packing of the product at point-of-sale accompanied by the promotional display and presentational follow-through.

Case Study

In mid-2006, the Hong Kong office of GolinHarris and long-time client Cotton Council International (CCI) set about developing an unforgettable "calling card" to help secure additional licensees of the COTTON USA brand—the primary goal of the organization. The objectives were to position COTTON USA as a premium brand, drive brand awareness, and strengthen relationships with industry influentials and the media.

The resulting *Evolutions* 2007 fashion calendar featured designer brands and cutting-edge photography packaged within a groundbreaking East-meets-West cross-cultural concept. *Evolutions* would win an international award for publication design.

For 2008, GolinHarris developed CCI China/Hong Kong's original concept of how US cotton—high-quality, comfortable, fashionable, and versatile—is a natural human companion for life's journey. Thematically, *Life Journeys* would be a celebration of life and its experiences. GolinHarris oversaw all aspects of production, including recruiting established and emerging talent between six months and 95 years old who mirrored the *Life Journeys* theme for the PR program.

(Continued)

The calendar was designed as "usable art," employing a vertical format typical of Chinese calligraphic scrolls and *shanshui* paintings, in comparable size. Elements of both the Chinese lunar and Western agrarian calendars were communicated in traditional and simplified Chinese as well as English. Garment bag-style packaging and a modern steel hanger enhanced the fashion element of the calendar, enabling owners to enjoy the unique piece of art as they would any other—by hanging it on a wall. And by featuring the fashions of CCI's licensee partners, the calendar highlighted the quality of US cotton as the key ingredient in delivering some of the world's finest clothing. The functional aspects, together with the fantasy elements of the art direction, created an effect seen in the best of today's fashion design.

GolinHarris and COTTON USA partnered to identify a charity that matched the ethos of the brand and also helped attract celebrity participants—who could in turn help drive awareness of the project. Care for Children, a non-profit organization operating to improve the lives of millions of orphaned or abandoned children in China, was linked to the project through an innovative Web platform allowing people around the world to donate to the organization by purchasing the calendar and downloading e-greeting cards and wallpaper.

Life Journeys achieved remarkable success. Over 47,000 wallpapers and e-cards were downloaded from the website, demonstrating the success of the site in driving awareness of the project. The calendar generated 119 media clips across Hong Kong and China. The premium quality of the calendar and the talent featured added significant depth and an essentially aspirational appeal to the COTTON USA brand.

Source: Golin Harris, Hong Kong.

Diffusion of Information

The sum total of the marcoms effort is geared to converting the existing and potential consumer from inactivity or ignorance about the product or brand to enlightenment, desire, and a long-term, happily-ever-after relationship as customer and brand gallop off into the sunset across the marketing plains forever. The role of public relations is also integral to, and relevant throughout, this diffusion of information process that underpins the customer relationship from getting the attention of the consumer to persuading them to buy into the brand.

There are several ways public relations can reach out with high impact to the Asia Pacific consumer on behalf of the product or service:

Alert/Draw Attention/Appeal/Attract: Attention-grabbing events, such as product launch parties, can be organized to engage the consumer.

Interest/Involvement: Public relations efforts can be geared to disseminating informational and factual messages to the consumer, to stimulate their interest about the product/brand in the form of targeted leaflets, advertorials, blogs, direct mail, e-mails, and editorial stories.

Evaluation/Assessment: The cognitive content of these promotional messages will supply the consumer with rational data on which they can base a decision. Would this product be useful? How will it help me? Here, the emotional content of the public relations message will stimulate desire and conviction to connect with the brand.

Trial/Try Out/Test: Promotional activities can be organized around incentives to stimulate the consumer product interface. This can be done for example, by handing out free product samples or product and corporate giveaways at events, in the media, on the street, or providing opportunities to try out the product at home pre-purchase by, for example, encouraging the potential consumer to test-drive a computer for the weekend in an attempt to stimulate a sale based on the premise that once they have been given something for free, they are more likely to buy into it.

Adoption/Accept/Take-Up: The promotional message should contain directive language and suggest purchasing action to encourage the consumer to buy into the product/brand/service/issue.

Brand Relationships

Branding lies at the heart of the consumer public relations and marcoms initiative in terms of managing the perceived value of the company or product name and how the customer as key stakeholder relates to it. The public relations effort in this regard is geared to ensure that the brand name breathes life into products and services and magically transforms them into attractive personalities from Singapore Airlines to the Hong Kong and

How Public Relations Can Lead the Marketing Effort

1. Organizing triggering events to attract the news media to cover the brand story

2. Brand-building in an incremental way to sustain the brand profile and develop customer loyalty

3. Monitoring customer perceptions of the product/brand and its competitors in the marketplace

4. Managing consumer relationships given the rise of more empowered, knowledgeable consumers

5. Creating awareness-raising events and publicity launches for new products/brands or repositioned ones pre- and post launch

6. Developing a positive image for the company brand—the big "B," behind the brand—the small "b"

7. Managing negative perceptions about a product/brand because it is unknown in the market or countering misperceptions about a nutritional product such as milk that has been associated with having a negative impact on health due to its potentially high fat content

8. Assisting with the protection of brand reputation during and after a crisis such as a product recall

9. Arranging sponsorship opportunities—connecting stakeholders with mutual interests to extend the promotional effort

10. Identifying relevant spokespersons or celebrities to promote the product/brand

Shanghai Banking Corporation (HSBC) or from SONY to 100 percent New Zealand. The intended outcome in this branding process is that customers will develop a meaningful and lasting relationship to the differentiated brand as if it were their best friend.

Turning fizzy water with sugar and vegetable flavoring into the most consumed beverage on the planet is a form of transubstantiation that owes so much to the marketing communications and public relations effort. Using sustained integrated promotional communications over a significant timeline, the generic product was built into a global brand inviting consumers not so much to quench their thirst but to relax, have fun, and be part of the global party. Branding is the way that a company and its deliverables are positioned in the market and communicate their ability to stand out from the crowd by promising to make a difference to the prospect's life.

Value of the Brand in Asia

Across Asia Pacific, the desire for brands appears to be insatiable and in certain demographic bands, such as the Gen Y Asian youth market, the fickle consumer is locust-like; flitting from one fashion or lifestyle brand to the next, devouring them up as they go and seemingly never repeating the experience.

This may be the symptom of immaturity and the endless search for identity, yet it reminds marketers that they must fully understand their target audiences' aspirations and their brand relationships. Consumers in developing economies across Asia, such as China, India and Korea, also tend to display this need to buy into premier brands as a badge of personal achievement and social standing as we saw in chapter 1. With increased education, greater access to digital communications networks, and concomitant global influences, Asian consumers may start to change their brand choices as a way of aligning with the sophistications of more globalized tastes and aspirations. Nevertheless, they will still yearn to define themselves through the multiple brands which they connect with, and buy into.

In other parts of the world and in countries such as Australia and New Zealand, consumerism is shifting its expectations from an expression of status through the brand, to finding greater self-fulfillment beyond the brand. In this case, the customer as stakeholder is demanding that the companies behind the brands openly demonstrate ethical practices in their operations in areas such as environmental and social practices. Here, the consumer wants to buy into a brand that aligns with their ethical value systems, such as promoting sustainable energy systems or supporting charitable causes, so that they feel reaffirmed when buying the company's products. In this sense, the public relations practitioner will be called upon, not only to develop and maintain the brand, but also to protect it through strategic issues management and crisis preparedness programs.

These trends are linked to the notion of the brand ethos itself. This is composed of the emotional values—the brand personality, the feelings the brand evokes in the consumer, and the rational aspects of the brand's functional attributes, including its tangible benefits. Both of these emotional and rational values should meld into a brand proposition that encapsulates the core of the brand's appeal to the consumer. The emergence of a brand conscience evolving out of these emotional values and the need to demonstrate ethicality is a new trend that will have to be increasingly managed by public relations and marcoms teams responsible for positioning global brands. This will be particularly pertinent for those companies located in more developed economies in Asia Pacific that are facing the fallout of an economic downturn and the related call for more corporate accountability in the market.

Point of View

"Doing PR in China is about learning to navigate the spectrum of interactions between businesses, governments, netizens, academia, media, investors, and consumers. In China, you've got it all: local companies trying to go global, global companies trying to be local; governments trying to communicate with the people, people trying to make friends with governments. And everything is covered in a heavy glaze of local culture. Making sense of these convoluted lines of influence is the challenge, and those that do so have found success in this dynamic market."

Scott Kronick, President, Ogilvy Public Relations Worldwide, China

---

Building and sustaining a robust customer relationship is the main focus of the marcoms effort and public relations is uniquely suited to achieving this goal. This strategic process is all about delivering consistently reliable products and services and fulfilling consumer expectations. Incentive and reward schemes so beloved by retail outlets and credit cards companies in Asia will assist in this. In addition, targeted media relations in niche markets are always beneficial in helping to keep the brand alive and relevant in the consumer's mind. Also, at point-sale or service delivery, the employee represents the brand and must consequently be well trained and display a positive attitude as this significantly impacts customer perceptions and is the site where employee relations and consumer relations overlap.

Public relations is capable of creating favorable and longer-term impressions on the people who matter most to the organization and its brands.

It achieves this because it:

- is highly adaptive, being able to tailor the communications effort as required in each situation

- has a great capacity to impact by creating drama and the buzz factor when launching new products, companies, or ideas through guerilla and viral marketing—mobile phone messages, social networks, interactive games, and e-books at high speed

- cuts through the clutter of messages and information overload by being relevant and on-target

- grabs attention using a range of media channels and reinforced communication messages

- provides credible information from expert, trusted third parties that enhance the prospect's understanding of company, product, service, and issue.

THE TEN CS OF BRAND BUILDING

1. Consumer—is king or queen, emperor or empress

2. Communicate—get the message out about the brand ethos and brand position to your target stakeholders

3. Contact—make sure that your message connects directly with stakeholders

4. Coherence—keep the same voice across all brand specific and corporate communication

5. Consistency—stick to a sole message, have a single purpose, and give a precise performance

6. Commitment—be totally bound to the brand throughout its lifetime so that your stakeholders will be too

7. Control—direct all that you do throughout the brand implementation program with helicopter vision

8. Clarity—have a clear vision of what the brand is and what you want to do with it

9. Cost—control and monitor the branding resource. This will depend on what the branding brief is. Launching a new brand will come with higher costs—enhancing an existing brand will cost less

10. Create—an impact, generate the buzz, and keep your brand as visible as possible to your audience at all costs

Business-to-Business Marketing

Sometimes dubbed the Cinderella of public relations activity, business marketing communications, or business-to-business, is not a hot topic for discussion in books about public relations. Sorry to say, this book is no exception. Maybe it is because business marketing is such a niche world of technical or specialist industries that do not directly affect wider audiences. It is often conducted behind closed doors or is only directed at a very small number of people. Yet it is a very important aspect of public relations enabling companies to function on a daily basis through the purchase of software, telecommunications, and building equipment, for example.

Compared with business-to-consumer relationships, the stakeholder groups targeted are relatively small; often involving those in an organization who are involved in a purchasing decision.

The PR effort will facilitate the sale of the product or the take up of services by writing the promotional materials for example. Here, the rationale for the business relationship will be founded on professional need and will be more functional as the buyers will be looking for a solution to workplace problems or issues such as increasing technical efficiency or speeding up productivity.

The specialist nature and content of the business communications interaction necessitates the use of specialist media and trade publications to get the message out about the product or service on offer within the specific field of business, be it sectors such as the building and construction trade, engineering, hotel management, or medicine. The majority of the public relations role in business marketing is played out through media relations—interviews and placement of news releases or, more typically, articles, advertorials, and feature stories in the specialist publications or the specialist sections of daily newspapers as they are specifically targeted at professional interest groups.

Other public relations activities would include educational seminars and factory visits for stakeholders such as industry analysts, exhibitions, and lobbying government departments for procurement purposes

Case Study

Lock&Lock, Korea's number one plastic container company, a relatively unknown brand when it entered the Chinese market in 2003, sought to firmly establish itself as an industry leader. The company harnessed PR's brand-building power by employing a multifaceted, long-term strategy focusing on exposure, emotional branding, and investment in socially-responsible initiatives.

The first step in PR firm Hill & Knowlton's strategy was to establish Lock&Lock's image as a premium brand by organizing a grand opening ceremony for its flagship store in Shanghai. The glamorous 2004 event attracted over 17 fashion and lifestyle media, generating extensive coverage highlighting its core "Keep it Fresh" message, maximizing exposure, and underscoring the desired brand image.

Following up on the successful launch and ongoing publicity efforts, Lock&Lock was then forced to deal with a difficult yet exceedingly common challenge in the Chinese market: copycats. The adaptive PR strategy was able to preemptively address the issue by creating a cohesive emotional thread between the brand and its superior product. The immensely popular Korean TV actress Yang Mi Kuang was strategically selected as the brand's media spokesperson to delineate Lock&Lock from local competitors and highlight the high-integrity of Korean manufacturing. A special autograph session with Ms. Yang to celebrate the first anniversary of Lock&Lock's flagship store resulted in its highest sales to date.

As China prepared for the Olympics, sports, health, and the environment were all prime targets for corporate social responsibility (CSR) efforts. Lock&Lock worked in concert with the National Sports Training Centre to support the development of local sports talent. Lock&Lock also sponsored a series of "Green Restaurant" events in partnership with the Shanghai and Beijing governments and the Olympic Committee. These actions not only cemented the brand's industry-leading image, but also strengthened ties with the government, an essential component of successful business in China.

Since its 2003 entry into China, Lock&Lock has transformed from a company with no brand awareness into a household name. Thanks to this concerted PR-driven campaign, its export sales have also increased 540 percent in mainland China. Additionally, Lock&Lock is now seen by influential media as a responsible corporate citizen as well as a friend of government, establishing a broad platform upon which to build in the Chinese market.

Source: Hill & Knowlton, Shanghai.

Endnote

1. Mercer, David, ed., *Managing the External Environment: A Strategic Perspective* (London: Sage, 1992), 44.

CHAPTER 7

The Role of Public Affairs in Asia Pacific

> **THE ORIGIN OF LOBBYING**
> The term "lobbying" is said by some to originate from the UK in the 19th century, where members of parliament frequently met with their constituents and delegations in the lobby area of the House of Commons. The US, on the other hand, has another account, and claims it began when petitioners would wait in the lobby of the New York State Capitol Building to address their legislators. Whatever its origin, the term lobbyist is common parlance throughout the world and in Asia Pacific in the corridors of legislative and judicial buildings from Tokyo to Canberra.

Public Affairs Explained

Everyday, elected and regulatory officials make decisions that could impact an organization's business—eat away at a commercial firm's profits or limit a non-profit foundation's ability to be effective. Public affairs' role is to anticipate when such a decision will be made, determine how to address the issue being decided, and develop an influencer program to make sure the decision is made in the organization's favor.

The way public affairs does this is to influence public policy through lobbying—be it private, aiming to influence a small number of people; or public, engaging in a mass media campaign and mobilizing wide public support.

Several different terminologies have come to mean public affairs—the generic terms government relations or government affairs were more popular in the 1990s—but they all fall under the public affairs banner. That said, we can also recognize the irony of these words, when we know that public affairs is sometimes anything but public.

Public affairs programs are often run like a political campaign, and many of them are actual political campaigns. The programs will utilize a diverse range of strategies and tactics, including research, alliance formation with industry or NGO groups, media relations, and grassroots and community mobilization.

Like all forms of public relations, public affairs seeks to create a dialogue within the political and social environment with the intent of having influence—either to make a change or maintain the status quo. It is all about gaining access to the right people and then making a clear and persuasive presentation of the case.

Direct and Indirect Lobbying

When we talk specifically about lobbying, we look at it in two ways—direct lobbying and indirect lobbying.

Direct lobbying refers to actually meeting and communicating with politicians and government servants, and providing them with information pertinent to an issue on which they have influence.

Indirect lobbying, on the other hand, enlists the help of other people and, often, the whole community, commonly called a grassroots campaign, working from the ground upward.

In a study conducted by the Hansard Society in 2007, it was found that UK members of parliament are approached by lobbyists at least 100 times a week. So if we take a look at an Asia Pacific example, in Australia there are 150 MPs and 76 senate members representing 21.5 million people. It stands to reason that they need to make informed decisions based on a range of intelligence sources and, based on the UK experience, will be lobbied about 22,600 times a week in total. On the whole, these 226 parliamentarians are prepared to listen to various points of view on an issue pertaining to a proposed legislative bill or government policy.

Like media relations, therefore, this makes it all the more important that whatever we present has to be compelling and persuasive. It is in the interest of government decision makers to base their decisions on a balance of views—to do otherwise may risk the wrath of pressure groups or professional and trade associations taking their story to the media and exposing negligence on behalf of the decision makers to fully understand the case and related interests, or a demonstration of unethical practices at worse. As citizens across Asia have become better educated and more information-savvy because of increased access to traditional and digital media sources, those involved in legislative and regulatory processes must ensure they keep their lines of communication open to a range of interested stakeholder groups.

Many public affairs firms or departments employ former political reporters, politicians, or government servants to help with the presentation of a case. With their high level of personal influence on current politicians, their personal knowledge is the secret weapon in many public affairs causes. In China, it is called *quanxi*—a personal network of connections and friendships, generally including public officials. What is needed is a good knowledge of the local political system, how legislation works, and who does what in government.

Public affairs often comes down to network contacts and timing. Again, in the parliamentary system in Australia, for example, legislation is hatched

Case Study

Davidoff had been engaged in a 25-year battle over its cigarette trademark in Indonesia. Trademark hoarder, Sumatra Tobacco Trading Company (STTC), had control of the Davidoff logo. Davidoff had to work in a climate of strong nationalism in the legal courts, with public opinion favoring local firms.

Davidoff hired public relations firm Indo Pacific after losing two related cases in Indonesia's Commercial Court, to educate the media on the necessity for the Supreme Court to be impartial, so that STTC's ability to work the court system behind the scenes could be minimized.

The program focused on demonstrating the international investor interest in the case, citing the dangers of the courts being seen as anti-international in terms of intellectual property law in Indonesia. In 2003, Davidoff was successful, and Indonesia became the site of the company's final legal triumph, with all countries now adhering to Davidoff's right to its well-known trademark.

Source: Asia Pacific PR Awards 2004.

and penned by the relevant government department and then passed to the parliamentary chamber for the review process. This means that to have any significant influence on the content of this bill, the related industry and business sectors should have early input at the ministerial planning stage to reflect their views about how a particular law will impact their operations. Knowledge of the legislative and policy-making planning processes is essential if an industry or a business wants to make its voice heard and have an influence in the lobbying game.

Elements of a Public Affairs Campaign

Organizations engaged in public affairs can range from major corporations to charities, educational groups and even overseas governments. The type of campaign they will develop varies from case to case, but there is a range of standard tactics that can be employed. Here, we look at the case of a fictional pharmaceutical company seeking to change the law to make its drug X legally available in the market. It will likely be implementing the following activities:

- Monitoring the issue and tracking its progress within government
- Devising a strategy which will raise the issue at government level and demonstrate why drug X should be made available legally
- Identifying key stakeholders in the decision-making process in national, regional, and local government bodies
- Running a public education program on the benefits of the drug via community meetings, blogs, a website, posters, and leaflets
- Meeting with influential politicians, government officials, and NGOs to lobby them on the proposed legislation
- Partnering with other pharmaceutical companies that have similar drugs, to form an industry coalition to lobby for the new law
- Developing NGO allies, such as charities that deal with the impact of this drug not being available
- Mobilizing grassroots—motivating individuals in the community to work together to raise awareness of the issue with their local politicians, via telephone, e-mail, and petitions

Case Study

Singapore Prison Service (SPS) launched its *Captains of Lives* (CoL) vision in 1999 to communicate its mission to provide rehabilitation programs, engage the community in rehabilitating inmates, attract new officers who embodied the CoL values, and reinforce the community's role in the creation of a stable social environment. The inaugural Yellow Ribbon Project was launched in 2004.

Burson-Marsteller (B-M) has worked with SPS since 2001, supporting various programs as part of the overall campaign:

- *Yellow Ribbon Project*—a framework for media initiatives aimed at "Unlocking the Second Prison" through community-involvement activities, also leveraged to highlight SPS rehabilitation programs
- *Media Relationship Center*—communicating SPS initiatives and rehabilitation programs, organizational excellence, and profiles of prison officers and inmate stories, helping SPS maintain a high profile
- *Issues Management*—tracking and managing issues and ensuring prison activities do not result in negative reactions amongst SPS stakeholders
- *Internal Communications*—developed and implemented a program to refresh the CoL vision internally and ensure all internal audiences understood SPS's vision and mission
- *Message Development and Media Training*—interactive sessions to refine SPS messages and train prison spokespeople

Over the years, the Yellow Ribbon project has generated substantial results. In a 2008 survey, 90 percent of respondents were aware of YRP and its objectives without prompting. More than 1,700 employers in the government's job registry, the Job Bank, expressed willingness to hire ex-offenders. There was positive endorsement by community leaders, including Prime Minister Lee Hsien Loong, and extensive media coverage in local print and broadcast media. Each September, some 350,000 Singaporeans don the Yellow Ribbon to show support for the reintegration of ex-offenders.

Source: Singapore Prison Service and Burson-Marsteller Singapore.

Despite the almost CIA-like secrecy that shrouds public affairs, its methods are available to all—the same skills used by a major corporation to influence the government can just as easily be adopted by local community groups. The local groups may not have the fiscal clout to carry their message beyond the local level, but often a local campaign is all that is needed.

The rising power of NGOs

One of the results of greater globalization has been its effect on non-governmental organizations (NGOs), which are becoming increasingly influential at a national and international level. Multinationals and other large enterprises are more engaged than ever with NGOs and consumer organizations; not only to persuade them as individual associations, but so that they can become allies in addressing a public issue.

For example, if an NGO such as the Philippines' Children's Rehabilitation Center or the All-China Environment Federation recognizes that the issue is one of public interest and relevant to their own mission, it most likely has greater leverage than a private company to move the debate into the public arena, engage in media outreach, and mobilize their own grassroots supporters.

Political campaigns

It would be hard to find a member of the electorate who is not aware that public relations and public affairs are key elements of a political campaign these days.

The chief public affairs representatives in a campaign are, in effect, the leading politicians themselves. They must establish a relationship with the public, with other politicians and influencers, the media, and, of course, the voters.

The US presidential elections of 2008 were, perhaps, the best demonstration of the power of public affairs—propelling a relatively unknown, African-American senator to fight an aggressive battle as the Democratic Party's candidate, to take on the highest position in the United States.

Role of Government Relations

Government relations experts or lobbyists function as the eyes, ears, and voices of the organization in that they monitor anything and everything of legislative and policy-making interest that may impact the organization and

Case Study

US-based non-government organizations worked with the Indian government, PSP-One, and ICIC Bank to tackle the issue of low sales of condoms in India. The lack of condom use has the potential to impact the country's health and economy. Yet, education was not the issue; it was tackling embarrassment.

Corporate Voice Weber Shandwick conducted pre-campaign research, which revealed that most people associated condoms with HIV and AIDS, and felt condoms were not for them, but only for high-risk groups.

A campaign aimed to break down the taboos associated with purchasing condoms, and a program to reinforce positive attitudes and behavior among young men, called "Condom Bindaas Bol," or "Say Condom Aloud" was developed.

The campaign ran across eight states in India and focused on bringing on board key groups, such as the media, celebrities and pharmacists.

As part of the media relations program, celebrities signed on to assist in developing public service messaging, while chat shows were created on a *pro bono* basis by partner media networks. The wider campaign also included consumer contests, viral video elements, mobile marketing, and social networking.

Since the beginning of the campaign, condom use across all target audiences rose 12 percent to 44 percent. There was also a 16 percent increase among the specific target audience who believed that condoms are for all people, not just high-risk groups.

Source: Asia Pacific PR Awards 2007.

advise their organizations how to respond to these developments or proposals. Lobbyists must have an in-depth knowledge of the legislative and policy-making processes, and also have a full and specialist understanding of the business and industry that they are representing.

The main tasks of the lobbyist or government relations expert are:

1. Legislative and regulatory monitoring
2. Using targeted media to convey the case for their issue
3. Presenting their organization's viewpoint to legislators and decision makers

4. Being recognized as a useful and expert information source for government bureaucrats and legislators

5. Regularly updating their organization on potential and existing regulatory or legislative initiatives in their interest field

Using controversy

Although public relations professionals have, sometimes, been referred to as the "lawyers in the court of public opinion," not all public affairs campaigns are carried out at a supreme court-type level. More and more, we are seeing public affairs at street level, employing controversy.

Creating a dispute or picking a fight is an effective way of influencing a target audience. Arguments and battles between political parties are the lifeblood of many newspapers and other media. So, controversies are almost guaranteed prominent media coverage.

The key to managing a public affairs "controversy" is to create a dispute that 100 percent supports the organization's public affairs goals, and is sustainable, so that it stands up even under the most intense pressure. If so, then there is a strong chance you will do well and have influence.

Why We Need Public Affairs

The arena of public affairs has become one fraught with conflict in recent years. Because public affairs aims to influence public policy, it receives more scrutiny than any other area of public relations. Many commentators are worried about the power that public affairs specialists or lobbyists have over politicians.

In the UK, there are several restrictions on what can and cannot be done in a lobbying program; not the least of which require all politicians to declare their interest with public affairs people and disclose the details of any agreements and fees they are paid. The US has even stricter rules, including prohibiting senators from lobbying Congress for two years after leaving office.

Similar conditions exist in all countries in Asia Pacific, where public affairs specialists need to negotiate with large and complex governments. This becomes even more difficult when working across a large geography. For example, in the Philippines, the government is centralized in Manila, but an issue may be a local one, in any one of the more than 7,100 islands that make up the nation.

Also, in this region, the majority of governments, such as Malaysia, Korea, and China, have strict protocols to follow in terms of how and when to approach government officials. One distinctive feature of China's business environment, its political system requires multinational corporations to practice strategic public affairs to interact constantly with the different levels of Chinese government, respond to the policies, and further influence business policy formation. A classic example was the Chinese ban on direct selling operations in 1998 and Amway's public affairs strategies to remove the ban.

While many politicians and government servants view public affairs lobbyists with, at best, suspicion, they are often providers of a great deal of research and data, which would have not been available otherwise. Also,

Case Study

During the middle of March 2003, when the SARS epidemic struck Taiwan and Asia, Taiwan's tourism industry was affected badly. Flights were mostly empty and there were few enquiries regarding travel, both domestically or internationally.

The travel trade and government departments led by the Airlines Association in Taiwan worked with Compass PR to turn the situation around and encourage people to travel again. Public confidence needed to be built in the health and safety of passengers in airplanes. The confidence campaign was named "Fly Taiwan, Fly," signaling both the need to boost Taiwan's economy as well as Taiwan's air travel.

The campaign kicked off with a launch and media event in June 2003. A two-day carnival was organized by airlines, hotels, travel agencies, and theme park operators. As part of the media relations effort, medical experts were quoted as independent sources for feature articles and news items.

Similar to other countries' efforts at the time, the culmination of the educational campaign and the gradual falling away of the disease prompted a comeback of business.

Source: Compass PR Taiwan.

we need to remember that lobbying is not only conducted by major organizations, but also by unions, welfare groups, and other worthy causes.

Public affairs is, indeed, we contend, the very essence of politics and public policies. Today, politics is all about communication. If parliamentary candidates, political parties, governments, and NGOs do not communicate their policies to their audience or have an open mind to the audience's submissions, then there can be no democratic process.

CHAPTER 8

Managing Issues and Communicating in a Crisis

The Cost of a Crisis

- 2007—over 10 million products recalled due to toxic paint used in China manufacturing
- 2005—international, branded café closed temporarily in Malaysia for serving non-*halal* food
- 2003—recall of 1600 health products in Australia, leading to the collapse of the company
- 2000—more than 14,000 people suffer food poisoning in Japan, resulting in a national product recall and a 45 percent drop in share price

---

What Is Issues Management?

A simple way to think about issues management is to consider issues as the gap between an organization's actions and what is expected by its stakeholders. Issues management is simply the process which is used to close the gap. It is the way that we can prepare an appropriate organizational response to those perceptions and issues that may impact its future. Issues management is like a form of insurance by planning for an eventuality on the back of issues.

When we consider issues management, we often think of multinational corporations, such as tobacco and oil companies, and pharmaceutical manufacturers, who face a barrage of criticism from specialist groups and the public. However, an issue could take any number of forms, including legislative or regulatory issues, an environmental or land use matter, a local community relations challenge, consumer complaints, worker safety, or investor confidence.

How issues are handled can mean the difference between an organization facing a crisis or achieving a proactive solution. For example, Master-Card implemented a successful youth debt reduction campaign in Taiwan, when it perceived that younger customers lacked the financial know-how to avoid credit card debt. In Hong Kong in 2002, the Hong Kong Jockey Club was quick to beat off successfully commercial soccer betting operations and persuade the government to legalize soccer betting only through the Jockey Club.

How we can manage issues

Of course, no one can actually "manage" an issue, and it would be arrogant to think so, as the term implies a level of manipulation. However, an organization can tackle an issue in two key ways:

- It can adjust its action to meet stakeholders' expectations. This could involve, for example, a change of corporate policy, new ways of manufacturing and service, or altered employee practices.

- Or it could seek to change stakeholders' expectations. For example, the organization may provide public education on the issue in an attempt to bring stakeholders around to the organization's point of view.

To be successful, issues management, has to be a genuine undertaking by the organization; not seen as just a "public relations ploy" or lip service to a set of values which is not truly embraced. Either way, it is important to take a reality check early on in the issues management process. The question should be asked if it is possible for the organization to actually influence the issue, and to what degree.

Several models have been developed detailing the methodology of issues management. However, when taken as a whole, there are seven basic steps to consider:

Identification

Identifying the issues which may affect or are already affecting your organization in the medium- and longer-term, with particular emphasis on the long-term sustainability to which Asian corporate leaders aspire. This could be done through a variety of means, including media and online searches, monitoring of specialist pressure groups, opinion polls, discussions with analysts and reporters, and monitoring of government and political debate.

Analyzing the issues

This will involve determining the likely outcomes or effect of the issue; if the issue is a long-standing one or a new kid on the block; does the issue belong to the organization only, or to multiple organizations; its field of influence—in terms of geographical and social reach; and the longevity of the issue—will it be over quickly or is it here to stay?

Analyzing the stakeholders

In tandem with the issues analysis, we need to look at the key players— who are most affected by the issue; what is their attitude toward the issue, how many are there; what is their degree of polarization; and whose opinion are they listening to now and whose will they listen to in the future?

Taking a position

The organization needs to determine what stance it will take on the issue—will you stand against the issue; will you take pre-emptive action; will you support the issue; or will you do nothing? These are all valid responses to an issue-based situation, and the consistent response commitment should come from senior management.

Strategy, messaging, and planning

A strategy and accompanying messages will then be developed, along with a plan to address the issues. The plan could include a range of activities such as public education, political lobbying, sponsorship, and discussions with NGOs.

Implementation

At this stage, the program will be implemented. The issues management program must focus not just on the outward aspects that will impinge on the organization such as the economic climate, but also should internalize the monitoring and scrutiny to what is happening inside of the organization in terms of financial policies and procedures for example. Organizations now, as a matter of course, are expected by their shareholders and stakeholders to be committed to socially and environmentally ethical practices and to demonstrate this in real terms beyond the annual report and corporate website.

Tracking and Re-evaluation

Continuing to monitor the issue is vital, and the organization needs to constantly re-evaluate its position and strategy as events move forward.

"There cannot be a crisis next week. My schedule is already full."[1]

Henry Kissinger

Facing a Crisis — The 30:70 Equation

There was a time in the 1980s when crisis communications was the most fashionable practice area of public relations. The process was surrounded by a fog of mystique, which only a few were able to enter. Nowadays, the mysterious principle are better known. And the truth is, from the public relations perspective, there is no mystery to crisis communications. Managing a crisis is 30 percent good understanding of the stakeholders, strategy, and messaging, and 70 percent common sense and some good luck.

When we think of crises, we often focus on the dramatic and catastrophic—the airline crash, the food contamination, the gas explosion. However, a crisis for an organization can often—and frequently does—start as a relatively small issue that grows out of control because insufficient attention was paid to it. Small technical faults, employee grievances, and letters from unknown pressure groups have a habit of biting back.

Public relations can play a vital role in crisis communications. But in reality, its role in crisis situations is not so different from its role on a day-to-day basis. Whether news is positive or negative, public relations is responsible for maintaining and improving an organization's relationships with its target audiences—via communications. In a crisis situation, this role is simply intensified and acted out quicker than normal.

In a crisis situation, public relations' goal is to get the organization through the situation with as little damage to its reputation and credibility as possible. It is even possible, by handling a crisis effectively, to improve an organization's reputation. Above all, organizations post-crisis want business to resume normally with no short- or long-term damage to the brand.

Crises often cause outrage and alarm, which means a rational explanation is not enough—the audience is responding with heightened emotions and the role of public relations is to appeal to these emotions.

With the rise of digital communications, the rules of the game have also changed. The media is now able to feed the public's appetite for shocking and fearful news, which it distributes with lightening speed to every corner of the globe. The advent of the Internet and mobile communications and their impact on public relations is discussed in detail in chapter 12.

Crisis Landmarks

Although every crisis situation is different and individual, there are certain landmarks common to all situations:

- *Surprise*—clearly a crisis will involve circumstances that have not been foreseen or could not be prevented. And, for some reason, they almost always begin on a Friday night...
- *Speculation*—once a crisis hits, rumors, speculation, and allegations start circulating and growing.
- *Limited information*—organizations are unlikely to have all the information they need in the early hours of a crisis. And, contrary to all instincts, important decisions will have to be made based on incomplete or unconfirmed data.
- *Escalating flow of events*—timelines are pushed forward and driven from the outside.

- *Loss of control*—the situation appears to be slipping out of the control of the organization into the hands of the media or special interest groups.

- *The fishbowl effect*—the organization finds itself in public view, with questions and demands coming from different stakeholders.

- *Short-term focus*—often organizations find themselves looking at the short-term future, which results in making quick decisions which may not be to the organization's long-term advantage.

In this book, we attempt to avoid clichés. However, at this stage, the "Asia hand" will feel duty-bound to tell you that the Chinese characters for the word crisis mean both "problem" and "opportunity." Please don't—it is over-quoted and now elicits a "so what?" response.

The 5Cs

The way in which an organization communicates with the media and other stakeholders during a crisis or incident is critical. Most experts in the field abide by the 5Cs principles:

Concern—the critical emotion to communicate in a crisis or incident. The organization needs to demonstrate genuine concern about the problem, concern about what has happened, and concern for the people affected now and in the future.

Clarity—the organization needs to communicate with clarity, and with clear and consistent messages. All spokespeople need to be singing from the same song sheet.

Control—as soon as possible, the organization must take control of the communications agenda and become the originator of all information.

Confidence—the organization must communicate messages with confidence, so the stakeholders are reassured or, at the very least, have an understanding of the situation.

Competence—finally, the organization should demonstrate competence, which reflects how it is handling the crisis effectively.

Three guiding principles

There are three principles that need to be considered when facing a crisis. These tenets are not altered by new technology, nor pugnacious pressure groups, or greater government scrutiny. They are, very simply:

1. Show that you are concerned about the situation
2. Tell them what you are doing to resolve the situation
3. And tell them what you will do to make sure it does not happen again

If an organization abides by these three principles, it will already have gone a long way to resolving its communication issues.

Having an insurance plan... and keeping up-to-date with premiums

Well-planned crisis and incident communications enable an organization to communicate effectively during a difficult situation, to a variety of internal and external stakeholders.

Developing a crisis management plan in advance is like having a comprehensive insurance policy. Most often, these plans are written up in the form of a manual, which is distributed to all relevant staff. The manual typically addresses the following areas:

1. Identifying Stakeholders   The organization needs to identify and collect contact information of all of the audiences or stakeholders it impacts on a day-to-day basis. These could include customers and clients, governments and regulatory representatives, NGOs, trade associations, emergency services, employees, and, of course, the media—and determine how much is known about them and if they are positive or negative toward the organization.

In addition to identifying them, as far as possible, an organization should establish a relationship with its stakeholders, so it can contact them quickly and, hopefully, they will give it the "benefit of the doubt" in the first instance of the crisis.

2. Scenario Planning   The next step is to conduct a vulnerability audit—assessing the range of possible crises that could occur; determining the probability of them occurring and the potential damage they could have

Case Study

Hong Kong's MTR Corporation has its fair share of days in the hot seat when train delays occur, regardless of how serious those train delays may be. But let's face it, that's the nature of its business and why it has assembled an impressive communications team that was primed and ready to go within minutes of an arson attack on a train on January 5, 2004.

At 9:14 that morning, a middled-aged passenger set fire to a bottle of paint thinner on the crowded train. Over 1,200 people had to be evacuated from the train station and 14 passengers suffered minor injuries from smoke inhalation.

While the company was dealing with the immediate situation, the corporate relations team swung into action, proactively informing the media what had happened and its impact on train service while sending a team to take care of the injured at the hospital. A few hours into the crisis, the MTR Corporation held a news conference to update the media on the attack, hosted by senior officials, along with representatives of the fire services and police. Later that day, the team arranged for the media to photograph the train involved and provided journalists with information to help them focus their stories on how the corporation's staff quickly and effectively reacted to the emergency. In the following days, the team continued to work with the media to highlight the safety of the railway system, and feed human-interest stories about employee heroism. This resulted in good media coverage and helped boost employee morale. Importantly, the team also maintained close contact with the Hong Kong government in order to pre-empt potential criticism.

Two days after the episode, Hong Kong's Secretary for the Environment, Transport, and Works sent letters of commendation to five employees, and the MTR chairman presented a passenger with a plaque for bravery in delaying the arsonist.

We often talk about turning a crisis into an opportunity—this is a rare, perfect example. The quick reaction of the MTR turned a potential disaster into an opportunity to showcase its highly effective safety procedures.

Source: MTRC Corporation.

on the organization; identifying trigger points for the escalation of an issue to a crisis; and determining the potential responses that can be made—both in terms of operations and communications. These scenarios will be dependent on the nature of the organization, and could be anything from product and manufacturing problems to labor problems, from NGO targeting to natural disasters.

3. Crisis Communications Team   It is important to identify in advance an "on-call" team of employees who will form the crisis management and crisis communications team. They should all know their designated roles and decision-making processes in advance; and know how to communicate with each other and where to assemble.

4. Communicating during a Crisis   Most crises plans have previously prepared messages, which can be quickly adapted for use in a crisis. The plan will also consider likely media questions and materials that can be distributed, including media statements, internal staff e-mails, advertising, website changes, and the activation of "dark sites" attached to the main corporate website.

5. Monitoring System   Effective monitoring of issues and potential crisis areas is essential to ensure the organization receives sufficient warning in the event of a crisis. The plan will include the establishment of a media monitoring system and access to regulatory and political news.

6. Simulations   Scenarios and manuals are, however, never enough. Many companies run simulations to test the plan and the team in crisis situations, which enables them to ensure the plan is up-to-date and understood by the relevant employees.

Communicating with the media

Crises are played out in the media every day. In some cases, the media is accused of adding to, or even causing crises. Whatever views we have on journalistic responsibility, we need to understand the media and the risks and benefits of working with them. We need to appreciate the media agenda, which in a crisis will be to look for a good story and search for cause and, possibly, blame.

Richard Mintz, managing director of The Harbour Group, is credited with, humorously, coining the phrase "Feed the Beast."

He said that the media is a "beast", which needs to be fed. He said news media has to eat all the time—it has an insatiable appetite and when crisis hits, the media's hunger only grows. So, he says, feed the beast, before the beast feeds on you.[2]

In other words, if an organization is silent and will not talk, the media will always be able to find those who are ready to comment and speculate. However, if the organization keeps up a steady flow of information, there is less room for third-party speculation and inaccurate reporting.

How Asia Used to Think

The issues that crisis communicators face in Asia Pacific are often added to by some of the more traditional views on communication. Some Asian companies look at the running of their business as their own affairs and feel that whatever information is given to the public is strictly the company's business. They resent what the media and the public may have to say about them.

This is, of course, an outdated practice. The era of saying "no comment" is long gone. However, when forced to the forefront, many companies still try to avoid speaking out. They may cite a variety of reasons, such as insufficient information, the legal implications, and the fear of revealing proprietary information.

In late 2000, a series of stories appeared in Hong Kong's major English daily newspaper, the *South China Morning Post*, accusing McDonald's of employing child labor in Southern China to make toys for its "Happy Meals." In fact, this was an old story by Hong Kong and China standards and will, no doubt, reappear on an annual basis for years to come. However, the story was quickly picked up by the major newswires and within days, was appearing on newspapers as far afield as the west coast of the US.

Both McDonald's and its supplier, City Toys, were cited. However, the response of the two companies could not have been more different.

While McDonald's went public on a daily basis about their processes and its investigation into the matter, City Toys simply shut the front door and would give the media no comment—resulting in speculation and publicity about City Toys' presumed guilt.

In fact, at the time, City Toys was fully co-operating with McDonald's to investigate the issue. However, by remaining silent, it allowed McDonald's to gain the initiative and channel the communication in a positive direction for the fast-food chain.

When McDonald's announced that they would no longer work with City Toys, it was too late for City Toys to recover the situation and, in fact, it had to close the factory in question. As for McDonald's, well, the power of the burger was stronger than the problem. One major newswire interviewed McDonald's customers outside a Hong Kong branch. The respondents said child labor was "bad," but it would not stop them from eating at the fast-food chain.

Sacrificing the Short Term for the Long-Term Benefit

Although it is public relations' role to ensure the most positive stance is put forward by an organization, many companies, from an operational stance, realize it is necessary to make a short-term sacrifice for long-term gains. Taking television commercials off the air, despite the monetary loss or admitting obvious minor culpability early on—the public "wringing of hands"—can offset much of the resentment.

An example is the Vitasoy affair in Hong Kong in the 90s, when bacteria were found in some of its soy milk products. Vitasoy leapt into action—in fact, Vitasoy was criticized by some for being too forceful—closing production lines and recalling millions of cartons of its drinks on the basis of fewer than ten complaints. But there is no doubt that the short-term losses paid off in the long-term. Consumer confidence was quickly restored, although the price was high in terms of lost sales and wasted production costs. Today, Vitasoy reports substantial profits and has expanded its presence to the US, Australia, and New Zealand. Would it have been able to do this if it had not taken such drastic actions back in the 90s?

Role of the CEO

The role of the CEO in a crisis is one of the most critical factors behind successful crisis resolution. Only the most senior corporate executive can really express concern in a way that both the media and their audiences will accept. Only a president or chairman, in the eyes of the outside world, has the authority to express contrition and to guarantee the correction of errors.

Pity the hapless marketing or public relations executive who is catapulted to the frontline to be the voice of an organization, instead of being a source of information. If he is not seen as having sufficient authority, he will simply find himself regarded as a "spin doctor" or the mouthpiece of an insincere organization.

> ### Case Study
>
> The Chinese government's response to the media reaction when the Olympic torch began its progress in March 2008 was a classic example of poor crisis communications. Human rights protesters pulled off a publicity coup in almost every international city on the relay and, instead of leveraging the upcoming Olympic Games, China's leadership found itself on the back foot and on the defensive.
>
> Then compare that with just two months later, how the government dealt with the aftermath of the tragic earthquakes in Sichuan in May 2008. Prime Minister Wen Jiabao provided us with a wonderful example of the role of the senior executive in a crisis. Within hours of the first quake, Wen was on a plane to the affected area and seen by the world's media at the scene. Back in Beijing, President Hu Jintao chaired an emergency meeting of the Politburo's Standing Committee and thousands of soldiers and police were dispatched.
>
> The Chinese government's action was in sharp contrast with neighboring Myanmar's slow and secretive handling of its devastating cyclone just ten days earlier.

Pressure groups

The political impact of crisis situations has been further reinforced by the growing strength of activist organizations. For special interest groups, it is not so much the factual evidence but their ability to raise emotions about an issue.

Crisis managers need to deal with these special interest groups who place pressure on organizations regarding their performances and work procedures. Pressure groups can even stimulate some crisis situations, the World Trade Organization (WTO) protests being a good example. If it should happen that the pressure group publicly identifies an organization as a "bad guy," this identification has a disproportionate effect to the actual circumstances. When dealing with a crisis, organizations need to factor in their motivations, be seen to be open, honest, and consistent in their statements and actions, and demonstrate a willingness to resolve the issues raised by the groups.

The Three Phases of a Crisis

This chapter looks at the strategy and techniques behind communicating in a crisis. It is, however, important to understand at which phase of the crisis you are in. Today's experts generally refer to the three phases of a crisis, as follows:

1. The response phase
2. The reassurance phase
3. The relaunch phase

Each phase has its own distinct approach to communications. The initial days of the crisis when the situation is being resolved, is called the response phase. The organization's role is to communicate frequently, with transparency and with authority. It is not a time to talk about the brand or future, non-crisis related plans.

The reassurance phase concentrates on reassuring stakeholders that the crisis has been contained and the organization is well equipped to carry on normal operations.

Often an organization will try to jump straight from the response phase to the third phase, the recovery phase. If the stakeholders and public do not yet have their confidence about the organization restored, and are not reassured that the company has done the best it can, then they will simply not accept any attempts by the organization to re-market itself. A premature promotional or advertising campaign can be a waste of money; it is key not to let your hard work fall on deaf ears that only want to hear reassurance.

Endnotes

1. "Kissinger: The Uses and Limits of Power," *Time*, February 14, 1969.
2. Richard Mintz, (then) chairman, US Public Affairs Practice, Burson-Marsteller, (speech, the World Air Transport Summit, 59th Annual General Meeting of IATA, Washington, D.C., June 3, 2003).

CHAPTER 9

Talking to Ourselves

Internal and Change Communications

Few companies would argue with the need to nurture and value employees as a vital organizational resource. They pay careful attention to managing the way that ideas, issues, and information are communicated inside the organization on all levels to reach and engage what might be considered to be one of the most critical, yet often overlooked stakeholder groups.

The public relations effort, often working with the human resources department, is geared to ensuring that employees throughout an organization are a key element of the communications flow within it. In this way, they should feel informed about organizational goals and missions, aligned with organizational values, and updated or "in the know" about new developments relating to organizational policies, procedures, and plans. All of this activity is premised on the idea that sound internal communications provides the base upon which we build effective external relations, and that a productive workforce is one that perceives itself to be fully incorporated inside the organization and kept fully in the communications loop alongside senior managers and coworkers.

Who are we talking to?

Many mission statements emphasize that the workforce is the jewel in the organizational crown and an invaluable part of the company. But, this pronouncement soon becomes reduced to hollow rhetoric if the sentiment is not applied in practice and essentially fails to demonstrate this to be a living organizational reality.

The relationship between employee and the employer is a highly complex one and is not as straightforward as it would first appear. The motivations as to why each side of the organizational equation is involved in this relationship need to be addressed as this will provide clues to where each is coming from, and what they want to get out of the workplace situation. This understanding will assist us in trying to develop an alignment of employee-organizational direction underpinned by good communication links so that ideally all employees are reading from the same page of the book.

Most organizations require that the workforce come to work on time, do a productive day's work, leave, and get up and do it all again tomorrow. They also expect the so-called skilled workers to deliver innovation and business strategy.

Meanwhile, employees want a fair economic exchange and appreciation for their efforts and, for many, the workplace is more than just a place to collect a salary. It is also a node of social interaction. In Asian cities, such as Shanghai and Tokyo, where living space is highly constrained—the workplace used to offer an alternative venue for interaction, which is why offices in these cities were still full of employees at 10 p.m. each night.

Whether the organization and, more importantly, the senior management recognize this will depend on the prevailing corporate culture and how it is managed. If we define corporate culture as "the way that things are done around here" based on as set of definable values—the behavioral expectations of the organization's senior management—often embodied in a company's code of conduct or ethics, we are close to the source. Clearly, conveying the organizational expectations to employees is useful and the intention is to protect the corporate brand equity and reputation externally. Yet, from a public relations and internal communications management perspective, this would only be part of the story.

You may clearly communicate the corporate mission and anticipated benchmarks of performance in codes of conduct, but a one-way flow of information, no matter how well crafted or brilliantly worded, will not necessarily get the right message across.

Given the complexities of employee motivations outlined above, we need to ensure that the persuasive messages embedded in these organizational communication missives are received, attended to, and acted upon for full effect. But if we want a sustainable engagement with these organizational aspirations—if we want to turn them into working reality and establish a credible reputation, they cannot just be imposed from on high as an imperial edict. We need to understand how employees interact with such messages—how they decode them and appropriate them into the organizational climate.

Throughout Asia, there are many managerial styles at play in organizations across the corporate landscape—private and public sector—small-, medium-, and large-scale enterprises—from family run companies to locally based multinationals. Taking account of all of these indigenous cultures and their way of doing things in the workplace has to be factored into every public relations approach—and not just when engaged with internal communications management.

MANAGEMENT STYLES BEHIND INTERNAL COMMUNICATION

1. **Directional**: employees are provided with information in a top-down, one-way flow with no opportunity for feedback. "This is what you do..."

2. **Educational**: employees are informed by line managers about what to do and are given reasons why this is the best way to fulfill work tasks in a downward, vertical, one-way flow. "This is what you have to do because..."

3. **Interactive**: employees are allowed to contribute ideas to senior managers and are invited to discuss organizational issues and their own work in a form of two-way communication flow. "Can we discuss what needs to be done here...?"

4. **Inclusive**: employees are regularly involved in a two-way communication flow that originates from bottom-up enabling the less experienced to share their ideas and contribute to senior management's direction. "What would you do about this...?"

5. **Involving**: employees at all levels are expected to contribute to the decision-making process. They are involved in bottom-up, top-down, and horizontal communications flows enabling workers' viewpoints to be equally represented and incorporated at all levels. "What do you think that we should do about this...?"

Communication flows within an organization are highly complex

The management style of the organization will determine the ways in which communication flows throughout its internal structures—top downward, bottom upward, sideways, or indeed if any significant communication actually flows in a direction at all.

It is worth noting that, in public relations, we are in the business of managing message exchanges that the internal, formal communication channels—such as newsletters, memos, and e-mails—can control and systematize. Yet, informal communication channels that exist among employees—such as the grapevine, often most active at the organizational "watering holes" of the photocopying machine, the pantry, or the stationery room—cannot be controlled. However, these communication conduits should be respected and encouraged by providing the physical and mental space for this site of message exchange as a way of contributing to a healthy organizational climate.

In this sense, the public relations internal communications task is to ensure that information, ideas, and knowledge are constantly flowing throughout an organization at all levels.

Different communication strategies will be required depending on the type of organization and its rationale. A company focused on delivering quality products with a competitive price tag at the lowest operational cost, will mainly communicate what has to be done to achieve this in a mechanistic sense. Alternatively, other more service-oriented organizations will highlight the need to develop and maintain good customer relations, having targeted their products and services at specific market segments. Here, transitional communication flow will be critical throughout the organization, especially vertically upward and outside of it to the clients being serviced and supplied, as feedback to all levels will be deemed critical to measuring success.

A communications audit is a good way of assessing the organization's current communication flows and the management styles driving them, in addition to an employee perception survey as a way of evaluating the effectiveness of the internal communication. Following this needs analysis, the public relations professional can recommend future ways of improving internal communications.

> **Case Study**
>
> Philips India's "Project Honeycomb: Building Employee Brand Ambassadors" was planned in response to a challenging period of stagnation at the company. The key objective was to instigate an upward shift in employee morale, and the company's corporate communications aspired to build trust, bridge operating silos, and help senior management become more open and accessible to employees.
>
> The project centered on the "Let's Chat" program, an interactive broadcast that had employees in 16 locations across the country interfacing with the Indian management team in real time via video streaming technology. In support of this was a range of initiatives, from "know our products" sessions, to medical checkups conducted in the office, plus "art of wellness" workshops.
>
> The program resulted in positive responses by personalizing the experience, as judged by a Gallup poll of 2,300 employees. The campaign was clearly money well spent, coming in at a cost of just US$5 per employee per month. "Let's Chat" was particularly effective. It built trust, making use of India's love of technology.
>
> *Source*: Asia Pacific PR Awards 2004.

What Difference Will Communication Make?

Internal communication needs to focus on matters of real interest to the employees if we are to get their attention, engage with them, impact their behaviors and align their values and aspirations with the corporate wish list—as we are once again in the "what's in it for me" zone here. Corporate news, policies, personnel matters, announcements, special events, and boast and brag stories should be angled from the employee's interest vantage point. Also, they should be communicated in a variety of multi-media formats—visually and verbally.

The selection of communication tactics to engage with employees will depend on the appropriateness of whom your target audience is, what you are saying as a message, and the organizational culture with its management styles and consequent communication flows.

Quite simply if you do not strategize your internal communication in view of these variables, then it will lack any purpose, or, in the worse case, it will be ignored and deleted by the recipient.

Face-to-Face Options: Meetings (large and small), workshops, seminars, team/departmental sharing sessions, briefings (group/individual), informal or ad hoc visits, social events and outings, exhibitions, presentations, and special events.

Distant Visual and Audio Options: Employee newsletter, e-mail, intranet homepage, websites, status reports, notice boards, display areas, and feedback schemes.

Distant Written Options: Video, webcasts, teleconferencing/Skype sessions, podcasts, e-mail, and blogs.

By paying attention to good internal communication management, an organization can contribute in many ways to overall organizational excellence by enhancing employee performance, encouraging employee involvement, communicating and aligning organizational goals and expectations with those of employees. It can also engender a sense of pride in organizational achievement, create a sense of *esprit de corps*, provide updated and timely corporate information, and prepare for upcoming issues, internal changes, and crisis management.

The Critical Management of Organizational Change

Change is an inevitability of corporate life if an organization is to remain adaptive and competitive in today's marketplace, and for the public relations professional, it presents many opportunities for creative initiatives.

When an organization is going though any type of change—the arrival of a new CEO; a merger, acquisition, or takeover; a rebranding exercise; an upgraded computer network; a new restructuring and consequent redundancies—then communication—proactive (providing information) or responsive (listening, opinion seeking, questioning)—will lie at the heart of managing these dynamic scenarios. This input will turn a potential issue into an opportunity for more positive visibility, information sharing, and engagement with stakeholders.

When faced with change, human beings invariably respond negatively as they are required to surrender the comfort zone of the status quo, which is never easy. In this way, the communications challenge is to persuade employees to view the changes ahead in a positive way and as one that will enhance their current workplace experiences.

Before implementing the public relations solutions, a needs analysis is required to review the situation ahead by meeting with senior management, getting the full picture, and developing key messages that will help drive the change process forward when communicating with employees at all organizational levels. This will assure a level of consistency of approach.

The following three questions need to be answered in preparation for employee engagement and to help prepare the key messages to emphasize the positive aspects of change and minimize the fear factor:

1. What is the rationale for the change?
2. What will be the impact—how will the change tactically affect employees' work patterns?
3. What is the personal effect on the employee?

This would typically start with discussion group-style meeting with those employees to understand their reaction to the proposed changes in terms of their concerns and ideas. Other ways of gaining feedback and monitoring perceptions among different employee groups would be surveys and focus groups which would provide more in-depth insights into how each level of the organization would prefer to be engaged in the change process and how they conceptualized it from their particular perspectives.

Major announcements about the change should come from senior management and be based on maximized face-to-face interaction with employees. This could take the form of interpersonal meetings with individual employees or town hall-style meetings with senior executives.

The key messages about the change should be sustained beyond the primary announcement and it should ideally percolate down from the top management to line managers as employees need to hear the same messages down the line from a variety of sources varying in rank. The same messages can also be sustained in a printed document distributed by e-mail so that the message is reinforced and can be consulted and digested by employees after the official announcements are made. In addition, the communications team should perpetuate open dialogue with employees after the launch announcements in order to encourage internalization of and buy-in to the changes.

Finally, as in all public relations programs, the change management process needs to be prepared for and evaluated. Ask employees to summarize the key message of the change process, ask them to evaluate the timing and the communications management of the organizational change, and whether employees felt that the treatment was justified and fair. The findings will feed into future change communication scenarios, which are effectively happening continuously to a greater or lesser extent in all organizations.

As a manager of internal communications or of organizational change processes, the public relations professional takes on the role of go-between linking up various groups of employees at all levels of the organization by informing them, incorporating them, and facilitating communication channels for meaningful exchange of opinions and suggestions to improve the way that things are done around here.

Case Study

An internal employee communications program and external branding campaign in China by Johnson&Johnson (J&J) focused on renowned, traditional Chinese scholar Lao Tzu's mantra, "One is the beginning of everything." This was developed into the theme, "One team, one Johnson," echoing the 2008 Beijing Olympics' theme, which J&J actually sponsored, of "One World, One Dream," thereby giving it contextual relevance. To maximize target stakeholder reach, short mobile phone messages were used in the initial stage of the launch campaign, followed by the creation of a theme song, which highlighted J&J's innate corporate ethos and brand values. Running for three weeks across the nation, the campaign involved nationwide events, a competition, and also showcased a music video. Employees at J&J were provided with collaterals elaborating the campaign including themed notebooks containing the lyrics of the theme tune, campaign visuals, J&J's credo, and a calendar. This employee communications campaign was praised by the judges of the Asia Pacific PR Awards because it built awareness of J&J's corporate values by aligning them in a highly relevant way in Chinese cultural characteristics.

Source: Asia Pacific PR Awards 2008.

Ten things to avoid in communicating corporate downsizing

1. Don't treat redundancies as if they are the only event taking place in the company. While not giving any less respect to those impacted, they should be positioned as an ongoing process in the interests of preserving the competitive viability of the organization.

2. Don't forget to prepare a rebuilding plan to re-establish trust and reconstruct the organization internally.

3. Don't keep managers at any organizational level in the dark about the plans for change—they need to know the information so that they can act as change ambassadors both in the meeting room and in the staff canteen.

4. Don't forget key stakeholder groupings—employees, shareholders, unions, families, clients, and local community. Kick-start your communications planning by identifying and involving them from the outset.

5. Don't minimize the impact of organizational memory; employees don't forget past experiences.

6. Don't ignore the grapevine as it is a critical source of employee reaction and emotion. Employ formal and informal research techniques here to ascertain employee reactions and perceptions.

7. Don't hide away; the CEO and senior management must be reachable at all times and not remote from the change.

8. Don't make the wrong employees redundant in the urgency to get the task executed. Laying-off valuable members of the team will send the wrong signals to employees in general and will undermine your rationale and key messaging.

9. Don't forget the survivors—manage their emotions, as feelings of anger, guilt, and confusion will emerge.

10. Don't confuse stakeholders by altering the change rationale midstream. Stick to the key messages throughout the change period for consistency and credibility.

CHAPTER **10**

Corporations Taking Responsibility

The Evolution of Corporate Responsibility in Asia Pacific

Pre-1980s
Charity
↓
1980–1987
Corporate Philanthropy and Sponsorship
↓
1988–1995
Corporate Philanthropy, Sponsorship, and the Environment
↓
1995 onward
Corporate (Social) Responsibility

It was not so long ago that the concept of corporate social responsibility (CSR) was unfamiliar in Asia Pacific. The nearest corporations came to it was giving charitable donations or sponsoring a sports team. The question then was less about how much good we were doing, but rather what type of publicity or hospitality opportunities we could get out of it. Even though the topic is now mainstream, it does not mean the challenges are really understood or adopted as business practice.

But expectations are changing. Increasingly, customers, employees, and regulators are looking for more integrity from companies.

What is Corporate (Social) Responsibility?

The term corporate social responsibility came into regular use in Asia Pacific in the mid 90s. It also goes under a number of other disguises—corporate responsibility (CR), corporate citizenship, responsible business, and even corporate social opportunity.

It is important not to confuse corporate responsibility with corporate governance, although the two are intrinsically linked.

Corporate governance is about the processes, policies, and laws that impact the way a corporation operates. All listed companies have to conform to one type or another of corporate governance, but essentially it is about ensuring the accountability of companies and company executives for their actions. Corporate law across Asia requires companies to demonstrate fulfillment of ethical, regulatory, and fiduciary duties.

There was a renewed interest in corporate governance in 2001, following the high-profile collapses of global firms such as Enron Corporation and WorldCom. In 2002, the US federal government passed the Sarbanes-Oxley Act (SOX), which put in place common standards for all US public company boards, management, and public accounting firms. Since 2008, of course, the impact of the global financial crisis has changed the corporate landscape forever, and many expect ever more rigid rules to be established.

Shhhh... SOX

While a major source of work for accountants, lawyers, and compliance officers, the Sarbanes-Oxley Act has been a convenience for communication professionals working with US-listed companies. Almost all data related to revenue and employees can be regarded as influencing the stock market and, under SOX, this information cannot be released, except in statutory announcements. So, when the annual rankings from PR Week and Holmes Report come round, instead of spending hours pulling data together, all communication professionals have to do is say "SOX" ruefully, accompanied by a regretful shrug of the shoulders.

Corporate social responsibility or corporate responsibility, on the other hand, is when corporations go beyond their statutory duties and consider the interests of society in the course of their day-to-day business. Organizations voluntarily take action to improve the quality of life for their employees, their families, their communities, and society at large.

We are now living in what is known as the "Responsible Century," a term coined by Professor Daniel Esty in 1997. The 21st century is expected by many to be the time that CSR takes a hold in business and in society at all levels, and becomes the norm.

There are three factors driving this CSR movement:

1. Growth of Activism   Seattle 1999 set the stage for the arrival of anti-globalization on most people's consciousness. The World Trade Organization (WTO) ministerial meeting was to have launched a new round of trade negotiations, "The Millennial Round." Instead, the meeting is now remembered for its major street protests and the first waves of truly international protest from special interest groups. This continues to build as each WTO meeting takes place; with over 1,000 NGOs descending on the host cities. Who can forget the sight of South Korean farmers jumping into Hong Kong's Victoria Harbor to swim to the conference and exhibition center where the meetings were being held in 2005? Two days later, on a Saturday night, hundreds of fellow members of the Korean Peasants League (KPL) brought traffic to a halt for over four hours as they walked through Wanchai shouting protests against the WTO and kowtowing every three steps.

NGOs like the KPL have been a key driver of CSR. NGOs are shining the spotlight on issues ranging from human rights and labor rights to the environment and sustainable development. With the rise of the Internet and wireless communications, both NGO and citizen activists have even more channels at their disposal to communicate their message.

That said, major international organizations such as the Asian Development Bank, United Nations, and ASEAN not only promote CSR but actively engage with corporations to foster major causes. For example, Visa International worked closely with the Pacific Asia Travel Association (PATA) to encourage tourism and the related economic re-growth in areas devastated by the December 2004 tsunami.

2. Corporate Governance Scandals   The erosion of trust in the corporate world following the financial scandals of 2002 forced companies to look at additional ways to demonstrate their ethical and responsible behavior. The rise in the number of CSR programs in the early 21st century has been partly attributed to the backlash of the scandals.

On the other hand, it will be interesting to see if CSR receives another boost following the financial meltdown in 2009, or whether there will be less money available for funding. The situation at Lehman Brothers is a case in point. Up until its demise in September 2008, Lehman Brothers had given US$39 million to global charitable causes from the Lehman Brothers Foundation; which included millions of dollars to Doctors Without Borders' relief efforts for the 2004 Asian tsunami.

3. Cultural Change   As each generation is born, so are new values and new expectations. While some of today's Asian youth remain oblivious to social and environmental needs, many of the mid-20-plus generation not only want a good product, service, or investment, but also expect the provider and their employer to behave ethically and socially responsibly. There is compelling evidence to prove this.

In 2007, Edelman Public Relations and StrategyOne conducted a survey on people's attitude toward the responsibility of corporations. They surveyed more than 5,500 consumers across nine countries, including 2,000 consumers from India, China, and Japan. They found that:

- 70 percent of people are prepared to pay more for a brand that supports a good cause in which they believe
- 56 percent are more likely to recommend a brand that supports a good cause than one that does not
- When choosing between two brands of the same quality and price, a social purpose is what would most affect consumer decision (41 percent), ahead of design and innovation (32 percent), and brand loyalty (26 percent)

The same is becoming true in the financial world. The concept of ethical and socially responsibly investments, an investment strategy which aims to maximize both financial returns and social good, is now well accepted by organizations and stakeholders alike.

What is at Stake?

The growing CSR movement has, in the past, drawn some criticism. The most well-known opposition was the renowned economist, Milton Friedman. Friedman famously declared that the sole business of management

Case Study

"It takes very little to "Give Life a Chance" so that critically ill children have the opportunity to live—like you and me."

Prema Sagar, Principal & Founder, Genesis Burson-Marsteller

Genesis Foundation (www.genesis-foundation.net) is a private trust, which facilitates critical medical care for abandoned and lesser privileged children with the intent and hope that such children may have an opportunity to lead a normal or near normal life and sustain themselves in the future.

The foundation currently works with several homes for abandoned and medically challenged children located in India in the cities of New Delhi, Noida, and Gurgaon.

In its ongoing work, the foundation took up the cause to raise money to save the lives of three little children—Gaurav, Vrundha, and Neethu. To support this initiative Ashok Nath, an employee at Genesis Burson-Marsteller participated in The Great Tibetan Marathon to help raise funds for these kids.

Through a communication outreach program the organization wanted to raise funds and awareness among the target audience to fund the treatment of the three children. It also wanted to raise the profile of the foundation in order that more people will donate to the cause of saving children's lives through medical intervention.

The communications sought to raise awareness for the cause—provide critical medical care for children in the areas of cancer, heart, organs, and extreme deformities. It was also important to communicate that 100 percent of contributions go toward treatment of children; trustees carry the cost of administration.

The campaign adopted an innovative approach to combine digital outreach tools with a strong media awareness program.

Ashok Nath's participation in the Great Tibetan Marathon was leveraged to garner financial support and aid medical intervention for the three little children. According to *Forbes*, The Great Tibetan Marathon is one of the world's five toughest marathons, which requires a great degree of mental and physical preparation. Each mile covered by Ashok in the marathon generated more funds for the needy children.

Ashok's marathon run was filmed and made into a "fly on the wall" documentary. The documentary was used by CNN IBN as live footage for a feature story on a group of similar initiatives.

Source: Genesis Foundation.

was to make money for its shareholders. He considered CSR a subversive doctrine.[1] Friedman was right... if we consider corporations as operating in a world filled only with shareholders. However, corporations exist in the real world; with customers, employees, community groups, local governments, and NGOs, all impacted by, or having an impact on, the company.

While the financial outlay can be large, the return can be even larger.

Companies conducting CSR activities are building trust in their organization, improving relations with their stakeholders, and attracting and retaining both customers and employees. Being seen as responsible is an important factor in how much attention a company receives when opposing or supporting legislative reform.

The phrase "social license" is often used in this context. CSR specialists believe that a company's very right to exist could be at risk if it is not seen to be doing the right thing for its community.

China is considered, by some, as the new frontier for the CSR industry in Asia Pacific. There has been increasing pressure on companies in China to engage in voluntary environmental reporting and disclosure by government departments such as the State Environmental Protection Agency (SEPA), the Ministry of Finance, and the China Securities Regulatory Commission (CSRC).

China's leadership status ahead of Hong Kong in CSR was reported by auditing and accountancy firm Grant Thornton. In 2008, among 34 economies surveyed globally, China recorded the highest percentage (74 percent) of privately held businesses having adopted CSR as a formalized strategy. In contrast, Hong Kong ranked 29th. Of course, the research could be considered slanted by the relatively new status of privately-owned companies in China, but it still tells a story. There is no doubt, too, that Chinese companies wanting to go global are realizing that they will have to put a focus on CSR as part of their effort to gain acceptability and build their brand. It must have been a big surprise for PetroChina to find itself targeted by global campaigners calling for it to divest in Sudan.

Meanwhile, the CSR agenda in Australia and New Zealand has traditionally been stronger than in the rest of the region. While CSR has not been driven in Australia by legislation, there have been two governmental enquiries into the role of CSR: the Parliamentary Joint Committee on Corporations and Financial Services and the Corporations and Markets Advisory

Committee. Both enquiries supported a voluntary, rather than mandatory, approach to corporate social responsibility—and in doing so, legitimized corporate social responsibility as an important commercial function.

The Trust Bank

Companies are now expected by their stakeholders to have a well-developed community profile and to have a broader view beyond the business should only be about doing business whatever it takes. Clearly, it is good business practice to foster and maintain positive and close relationships with the community in which the organization functions. The wider societal push for responsible and responsive business practices should align with all that the company stands for and achieves on the premise that by contributing to society and the wider environment, an organization is ultimately raising the bar for every stakeholder. In fact, CSR should run throughout all levels and functions of the company's internal and external operations including R&D, production, finance, personnel, and marketing.

The benefits of this more socially responsible and community oriented approach can be evaluated in terms of building a "trust bank" of goodwill for the organization. These credits that are deposited for community-based contribution should reinforce the brand, engender stakeholder respect, and also provide a buffer against the negative feedback that emerges during the inevitable crises that every organization faces at one time or another. The hope being that if you have a healthy bank account of community and CSR credits, then stakeholders and the media will be more forgiving when things go wrong and more understanding of the circumstances.

Three Areas of CSR

The practice of CSR falls into three main categories:

Environmental

As recently as the mid 1990s we used to advise Hong Kong and Singapore companies against using the environment as a platform for philanthropy or promotion. "Green doesn't sell," we said. It was also considered risky for companies to talk up the environment as a cause; if they promoted their green accomplishments, maybe they would find themselves ridiculed later for other not-yet-known environmental problems.

This has changed. Today, recognition of the impact we have on the environment has moved to both the political and business platforms, and become an everyday discussion item on the board meeting agenda.

In May 2007, research conducted by CSR Asia and the Centre of Urban Planning and Environmental Management at the University of Hong Kong looked into which factors were the most important to Hong Kong businesses and their stakeholders in determining what makes a company socially responsible. The 15 factors they chose ranged from health and safety, human rights, and the environment. Good environmental performance was a clear winner, ranking first among the 15. How times change.

With discussion on climate change becoming the norm, the greening of public relations reflects the new reality. Corporations are becoming more public about their environmental goals and initiatives, even if they're less than perfect.

Many countries in the region are working to reduce their own pollution levels and become carbon neutral. WPP, one of the world's largest communications services groups, with around 1,000 offices in Asia Pacific, announced it had become carbon neutral at the end of 2007. It had been reducing carbon dioxide emissions by an array of methods—from installing motion sensitive lighting and increasing video conference facilities, to reducing air travel and purchasing carbon offsets from renewable energy systems.

The *Straits Times* reported last year that Singapore and close rival Hong Kong are "neck and neck" to claim the title of Asia's carbon trading hub. Both cities have established legal frameworks to allow companies to buy and sell carbon credits. ecoWise's subsidiary, Bee Joo Industries, was the first company to do this in Singapore—selling Japan's Kansai Electric Power Co. up to 95,000 carbon credits, equivalent to the reduction of 95,000 tons of carbon dioxide. Bee Joo is able to generate its credits through various projects, including the drying of waste, such as spent grains from breweries, which result in the saving of 6.1 million liters of diesel every year (www.ecowise.com.sg).

Of course, the main challenge when addressing environmental issues is that they keep shifting. Consider bio-fuels. They have gone from being regarded as a future energy solution to being seen as a cause of more deforestation and loss of livelihoods.

Social

As a result of globalization, we have become increasingly aware not only of what we buy, but also how the goods and services we buy have been produced. Child labor, dangerous working practices, and other in-humane conditions are examples of issues being brought into the open. We only have to think of the spate of factory labor scandals in the 90s and, more recently, the rescue of more than 100 children from factories in the city of Dongguan, China,[2] and the violation of workers' rights including poor living conditions, wage deductions, and withheld pass-ports in Malaysian contract factories for a sports manufacturer in 2008,[3] to understand why governments and the public are demanding that they must act in accordance with norms of right and wrong. Companies seen to be driving the improvement of working conditions and local commu-nity facilities have a head start.

India has a long tradition of paternalistic philanthropy. Large firms such as Tata are particularly active in providing social services, including schools and healthcare, for local communities. Tata Steel also has sophisticated community-based projects ranging from "adopting a village" in poor rural areas to protection of communities around the locations of plants.

Economic

Companies are increasingly looking at job creation and how they can ensure they are inclusive in their employment practices by helping disad-vantaged groups in the labor market and promoting lifelong learning, which increases employability and brings about poverty reduction.

Tata, again, has put a particular emphasis on affirmative action, especially in relation to ethnic minority communities and women.

Partnership with Public Relations

Public relations plays a significant role in communicating the socially responsible activities of a corporation. In many companies, the CSR role either falls within or works hand in hand with the communica-tions department.

There are many ways public relations is supporting the CSR agenda:

- Helping corporations develop their corporate responsibility policy, including company principles and codes.
- Building NGO and community relations.
- Linking CSR initiatives to corporate reputation and brand positioning efforts.
- Implementing media relations programs targeted to key external stakeholders on policy commitments and performance.
- Building employee communications and training programs to drive understanding and commitment to CSR.
- Communicating commitments with suppliers and vendors.
- Organizing volunteer programs to support the main CSR direction.
- Conducting community meetings as a means of consensus building for addressing and reporting on CR issues.
- Preparing corporate responsibility and other social/environmental reports.

Should we promote our CSR?

There is much debate in the boardroom and in marketing and communications departments on whether you should promote CSR activity. Some companies are wary about talking up their CSR activities, fearing they will appear exploitative. The "greenwash" backlash of the 1990s scared many CSR practitioners away from public relations. Companies' environmental credentials were exposed as decidedly lacking and many companies are now afraid to risk sticking their head above the parapet.

But, if your competitors are talking CSR and you do not, consumers and investors will assume that you are doing nothing at all. The public needs to know what a corporation is doing and how it is responding to societal issues, so they can make an informed choice. It also allows companies to show their human face.

We need to go right back to the beginning of this book and consider our "Acknowledgment of Achievement" principle, to know that we should not be afraid to use CSR as a marketing tool.

Mind you, we need to manage expectations. Companies should not expect the media to rush to print with a story on how the company

Case Study

Money skills are among the most important skills for a successful, happy life. But most schools don't teach this. According to research by the Hong Kong Institute of CPAs, most parents are not confident in their ability to teach their children basic money management. The Hong Kong Institute of CPAs saw an opportunity to reach Hong Kong families with a core skill of accountants—money management. Through its "Rich Kid, Poor Kid" program, CPAs volunteer their time to conduct road shows for secondary schools (teenagers) and storytelling sessions for primary schools (children eight to 12 years old), with involvement from their parents. These volunteers are supported by a broader campaign run by the Institute.

The program strategy aimed to align the core skills of CPAs with a gap in teaching curriculum, use the institute's "Accountant Ambassadors," and demonstrate the institute's brand promise of CPAs being a "success ingredient" in business and society. The institute commissioned an author to create "May Moon," a little girl who with her talking book leads children on an amazing adventure like no other in *May Moon and the Secrets of the CPAs*. For parents, it published *How to Raise a Money-Wise Child*, available in a box set with *May Moon*.

The program began in 2005 and, by the end of 2008, had reached 20,000 school children. It has created a stronger tie between the 800 Accountant Ambassadors and the Institute, which is a significant proportion of the 27,000 membership.

Media coverage of the program and the research behind it has been impressive, reaching about 10 million news-readers and viewers in Hong Kong. The coverage boosts the credibility of the program and maintains the excitement of the Ambassadors. Evaluations from schools' principals or teachers are excellent, with full marks given. Almost 9,000 books have been distributed in schools with about 850 sold in bookstores. The book sets have been translated into Chinese (by the Hong Kong Institute of CPAs) and Dutch (by the Royal NIVRA). Versions for Scotland and Canada are in the works, which will be completed under the auspices of those national institutes.

Source: Hong Kong Institute of CPAs.

recycles its office paper. Also, just writing words about how your company is committed to (fill in country name) does not cut it these days. There has to be substance behind the declaration.

"Triple Bottom Line" Reporting

Triple bottom line or corporate responsibility reporting simply means expanding the traditional reporting framework to include environmental and social performance in addition to financial performance. The phrase was first coined by CSR pundit John Elkington in 1994. He later expanded on the concept in his 1998 book *Cannibals with Forks: the Triple Bottom Line of 21st Century Business*.

There are no set formats for this type of reporting as yet; most likely because it is difficult to indicate the impact of a CSR program on the community or the company. This means that today's reports are a wide and varied bunch. Reports range from special sections in an annual report to stand-alone brochures. Several companies in Asia Pacific are currently producing CSR reports, including Hong Kong's Cathay Pacific,[4] Korea's LG,[5] Japan's Sony,[6] and Australia's Telstra.[7]

In fact, corporate responsibility mentions increased 18 percent from 2003 to 2007 in CEO letters to shareholders, according to research conducted by global PR firm, Weber Shandwick. In its report, "Planet 2050 On the Minds of CEOs" it says that Global 100 CEOs' communications on corporate responsibility initiatives have increased in the last few years. It says that in 2007, energy efficiency and carbon emissions were the dominant corporate responsibility initiatives addressed in CEO letters to shareholders. Yet, these topics barely garnered a mention in 2003.

The Four Principles of PR and CSR

We have honed down to what we see as the four most important areas to address when conducting public relations efforts for a CSR program:

1. **Reality over rhetoric.** While communications is critical in helping the audience understand the good being done, the initiative has to be demonstrably real and tangible.

Case Study

Since its entry into the China market 20 years ago, Audi has been an active corporate citizen through sponsorships and charitable donations. Audi wanted to transcend this role by setting a new benchmark for corporate social responsibility programs in China. Teaming up with UNICEF and its official implementation partner in China, the China Association for Science and Technology (CAST), Audi aspired to achieve a long-term and large-scale program helping children in poverty-stricken areas of Western China realize their dreams.

On December 15, 2005, the UNICEF/Audi "Driving Dreams" program was created to sponsor learning centers for out-of-school children in rural areas of Western China, providing free life-skills training, computer equipment, counseling, and sports activities/equipment in hopes of encouraging at-risk children to achieve their full potential. The goal is to reach children in 140 villages spread across 10 provinces in Western China.

Audi, along with its PR firm, Ruder Finn, concluded that in order to achieve the objectives of a sustainable CSR program, it cannot solely be based on traditional corporate donations, but has to fund itself over time and impact less-developed areas. Audi's strategy involves a five-year timeline (2006–2010) with a sustained financial commitment. Audi committed to donate US$100,000 each of the five years to the learning centers. Public awareness was raised by a multi-pronged media relations campaign targeting business, automotive, educational, sports, and lifestyle outlets.

Since its inception, 300,000 people have participated in the Driving Dreams program. The program has raised charitable donations of RMB 7 million and organized nearly 10,000 sporting events as well as run life-skills training at 140 learning centers across the nation. According to a UNICEF China Representative, "Audi China is a shining example of the rapidly developing field of corporate social responsibility."

In addition to Audi's Driving Dreams CSR program, Audi and their partners were among the leading corporate donors to UNICEF to give emergency relief for children and families affected by the Sichuan Earthquake, raising RMB13,061,924 (US$1,900,000). Over 124,000 children within the most severely affected areas of the Sichuan Earthquake benefited from emergency supply intervention provided under Audi Special Relief Fund's support. *Business Watch* magazine stated that, "Through its collaboration with UNICEF, Audi has established a milestone in CSR practice."

Source: Audi and Ruder Finn.

2. **Choose your cause wisely.** Ensure you focus your efforts on a cause where you can make a real difference.

3. **Show senior support.** The company's leadership team should be visible at all times. Their involvement will be taken as a sign of how important CSR is to the company—whether it has genuine support or is just mere window dressing.

4. **Engage employees.** A company should not only communicate externally. Employees who know that their company is committed to CSR can become its most powerful ambassadors. Companies that have successful volunteer programs tend to have better rates of recruitment and retention.

Corporate Response to the Asian Tsunami

On December 26, 2005, a massive earthquake shook the sea floor off the coast of Indonesia. Within an hour a giant tsunami had struck the province of Aceh, and over the ensuing hours it had hit India, Sri Lanka, Thailand, the Maldives, Malaysia, Myanmar, and Somalia. With at least 226,000 dead or missing and 1.7 million displaced, the scale of the disaster was unprecedented in recent history.[8] UNICEF estimates that over a third of those who perished were children.

The tsunami is an example of an international issue that needed an immediate and large-scale response. Anecdotal evidence from the media and multilateral organizations such as the United Nations (UN) indicates that corporations were key players in the tsunami response efforts and their donations were a vital element of relief programs.

Numerous companies made immediate and ongoing corporate and staff donations to help the relief efforts. China National Petroleum Corp. donated US$627,490 to Thailand and Indonesia, COSCO donated US$1.2 million to the China Red Cross, giant carmakers Toyota Motor Thailand and Asian Honda Motor each pitched in nearly US$300,000 to help the southern victims.

Donations were not all in the form of cash. Cathay Pacific provided free flights for emergency aid and held in-flight collections, Huawei Technologies sent telecom equipment, and Bristol-Myers Squibb shipped medicines as well as giving US$1 million to the Red Cross. MasterCard waived fees for contributions made by US cardholders to the American Red Cross's tsunami relief fund and worked with the US federal law enforcement to help prevent Internet donation scams related to tsunami relief.

Manulife Indonesia tragically lost 15 members of its staff along with their 11 spouses and 35 children. In the immediate aftermath of the disaster, it set up two refugee homes. Vehicles were hired to ferry people to their safe haven in Medan and were used on return journeys to carry food, water, clothing, and medical supplies. In addition to emergency fund relief, Manulife held its first global fundraiser, the "ACTION Aceh Relief Fund," which included donations from three continents and raised over US$500,000.

The success of the corporate response is clear to see. They have helped—and continue to help—restore areas into flourishing, financially-stable communities.

Corporations continue to look beyond current needs and to the future. Business entities across the Asia-Pacific region have formed partnerships with communities in tsunami-hit areas not only to help restore local economies but also to prevent future disasters. DHL, for example, is working with the government of Sri Lanka to support future disaster response by supporting leadership in the handling of humanitarian relief cargo.

Since the tsunami we have, of course, experienced the terrible tragedy of the earthquake in Sichuan, China. Similar to the tsunami, international companies rushed to give aid—giving funds and on the ground support for immediate relief and rebuilding. For example, New York Life International is engaged on rebuilding a school; partnering with the Sichuan Youth Development Foundation and the Hope Foundation.

Source: DHL—*Asian Tribune,* October 30, 2008; Manulife—http://www.manulife-indonesia.com/Aceh_All.htm; general donation data—Association for Sustainable and Responsible Investment in Asia—http://www.asria.org/ref/library/others/tsunami/1105504784.

CSR is a wonderful opportunity for companies, but can also be a risk if not handled properly. A CSR program which does not have company-wide support and is implemented only at its barest minimum will be seen as purely a "PR activity." Badly managed CSR can generate serious damage to a company's reputation, and consumers can act against companies that do not show genuine socially respectful behavior.

We need to recognize that engaging in CSR is an opportunity, not a sacrifice. Most importantly, of course, it is an opportunity to change the future for the better. But it is also an opportunity for companies to build goodwill with customers and investors, anticipate market and governmental pressures, and, let's face it, improve the bottom line.

Corporate social responsibility is not just about doing "good PR." Public relations is, however, an essential element. By communicating their efforts, we can help companies maintain credibility and build trust with their stakeholders. This is our mandate—demonstrating how companies and industries are creating economic value while building a more sustainable world.

Endnotes

1. Friedman, Milton. "The Social Responsibility of Business is to Increase its Profits," *New York Times Magazine*, September 13, 1970.
2. Barboza, David, "Child Labor Rings Reach China's Distant Villages," *New York Times*, May 10, 2008.
3. Levenson, Eugenia, "Citizen Nike," *Fortune*, November 17, 2008.
4. https://www.cathaypacific.com/cpa/en_HK/aboutus/csreport.
5. http://www.lge.com/about/sustainability/social_responsibility.jsp.
6. http://www.sony.net/SonyInfo/Environment/ForTheNextGeneration.
7. http://www.telstra.com.au/abouttelstra/csr/reports.cfm.
8. Bray, M., "How Safe is the Indian Ocean now?" *cnn.com*, June 27, 2005, http://edition.cnn.com/2005/WORLD/asiapcf/06/24/tsunami.alert/index.html.

CHAPTER 11

The Big Three—Investor Relations, Healthcare Communications, and Technology Communications

This chapter looks at three of the largest and fastest growing public relations practices; investor relations, healthcare communications, and technology communications.

Investor Relations: Show Me the Money

"The safest way to double your money is to fold it over twice *and put it in your pocket*."

Frank McKinney Hubbard

As in any field of public relations, the financial media and investors do not like to be kept in the dark. Lack of communication or mis-communication can have a ready impact on share price. A company that does not engage with the media can find itself under attack. Information moves markets.

The overriding aim of investor relations (IR) is quite straightforward: it is to ensure the lowest cost of capital and the highest sustainable price for a company's shares. A strong share price is a powerful asset for any company in acquisition mode and, on the defensive side, good preventive medicine if a company is an acquisition target. In simplistic terms, the role of a public relations practitioner is, therefore, to create positive communication between investors and publicly traded companies.

Open, transparent, and timely communication from investor relations teams support the reputation of a company. The benefits are apparent—companies can build long-term shareholder value, experience decreased stock volatility, increase liquidity, and have a lower cost of capital.

Communicating a transaction—that is an agreement between a buyer and seller to exchange an asset for a payment—is also about gaining its acceptance while maintaining normal business operations. Initial public offerings (IPOs), mergers, acquisitions, restructurings, hostile takeovers, bankruptcies, divestitures, leveraged buy-outs, and other corporate financial transactions have their own complex communications requirements. Effective communication during these times is critical in order to position a company with its stakeholders, including current and potential shareholders, regulators, analysts, rating agencies, and the business and financial media.

The world of investor relations has become more complex in the last decade. Stock markets and other financial markets have become more interdependent; investors in Sydney can equally invest in the Bombay Exchange or the Hong Kong Stock Exchange. Thus, if engaging in a foreign listing (see IPO), management has to consider many different factors, including time zones, languages, and format and, or course, local regulations. The 1990s also brought with it the revolution of Internet banking. People who never dreamed of buying shares can do this daily as they log on to their online investment accounts. In most Asian countries there has been a proliferation of online brokers, such as Charles Schwab, as well as the major banks, such as HSBC, offering online trading.

The same technology that enables the internationalism and complexity of the markets has, however, also eased the task of investor relations, as we can now provide timely, convenient access to company background, reports, filings, and news on websites, and e-mail to stay in daily touch with analysts, investors, and the news media.

When the going gets tough

In tough economic times, financial communications is more important than ever. When times are good, the need for public relations may seem small because—the money keeps rolling in. Yet, when times get tough, companies should reassure investors that their money is safe. The meltdown of the stock markets and critical investor response of the 1990s brought with it a wave of new regulations and an insistence on more corporate governance and disclosure. The 2008-09 economic crisis will certainly usher in a new phase of financial regulations that will radically change the financial landscape and impact public relations activities in this sector.

Financial markets have always been cyclical, moving regularly between "bull' (prices generally moving upward) and "bear" (prices falling). Many practitioners in Asia Pacific have never worked in a bear market. Some found the economic downturn of 2008/09 a whole new ball game.

Essentially, there are just two potential messages in a financial downturn:

1. The organization is financially secure, has strong management, and is committed to its customers and shareholders.
2. The organization is doing its best to resolve any issues, and is committed to its customers and shareholders.

While performance and financial data are critical to communications at these challenging times, of course, they are only two parts of the parcel that needs to be demonstrate the attractiveness of a company or stock. As discussed in chapter 5, non-financial factors such as the CSR policy of a company, its employee practices, and the status of the CEO play a major role. This is time when the CEO should be more visible than ever; when every opportunity to demonstrate positive action and stability should be taken.

> The Sarbanes-Oxley Act (SOX) of 2002 increased significantly the importance of investor relations. SOX established new requirements for US-listed companies with regard to compliance and regulatory governance, with an increased emphasis on accuracy in auditing and, of special interest to investor relations, public disclosure.

Who are we talking to?

Shareholders, be they institutional or individual, are, of course, the key target for the financial communicator. However, investor relations practitioners also need to address those who influence the shareholders. These include major banks and financial institutions dealing with large corporate and individual clients; analysts who specialize in particular industries, usually working in major banks and financial institutions; politicians and government regulators; employees; and, of course, the business and financial media.

The role of an investor relations practitioner

On a day-to-day basis, much of investor relations work is fairly routine—albeit vital—utilizing a range of financial tools and techniques available. There is a defined calendar for listed companies, when certain activities should take place. These include the interim or half-year results, the preliminary announcement of the full-year results or prelims, the publication of the Annual Report and Accounts, and the shareholders' Annual General Meeting (AGM). These announcements offer perfect opportunities to get the message out and establish stronger ties with financial audiences.

Here are some of the most customary activities for an investor relations professional:

- Annual General Meeting (AGM)—the public relations tasks involved in the preliminary announcement include preparation of the chairman's statement, development of the announcement media release, notification of the results to the stock market, and issuance of the media release to the media arranging briefings for the CEO and CFO with analysts and financial media.

- Annual report—the key document, which, by law, has to be produced by all public companies. The report has many different roles—not only dealing with annual financial results but acting as an introduction to the company's services and products, and as a reassurance for current investors.

- Interim results and pre-results "alerts." Also financial books, which provide more detail on financial performance and are particularly useful for analysts who need to fully understand the operating environment in which the company works.

- Preparation of speeches for the CEO and CFO for delivery to financial audiences.

- Road shows and one-on-one meetings with key financial institutions, shareholders, and analysts. Companies can have the opportunity to present their own analysis of performance and prospects. With increased costs and reduced time available to company officials, they are often being replaced by quarterly and semiannual video conference calls and live Internet webcasts, whereby the company officials can meet with their audience virtually rather than in person, present their company, and answer questions in real time.

- And, of course, on-going dealings with the financial and wider media.

Financial media relations

Financial media relations is aimed at a relatively small but influential group of reporters. Even in Asia Pacific, global media such as the *Financial Times,* Reuters, Dow-Jones, and the *Wall Street Journal Asia* are critical targets for investor relations, topping the major national daily newspapers.

However, communicators should be aware that other audiences are interested in the company's performance—in particular a company's employees. Trade media and regional media are often targeted as well, in order to reach these wider interest groups.

Observing rules on confidentiality is of course very important in the financial market. There are complex rules and regulations governing financial communications; each stock market in Asia Pacific has its own set. There are periods of "dead time," when constraints are imposed on the release of price-sensitive information. However, there remain many months when there are no statutory communication requirements and companies are free to engage in media relations activity.

A LOOK AT LISTINGS

A company has an initial public offering (IPO) by issuing shares to the public for the first time. IPOs are frequently held by younger companies seeking capital to expand or privately-owned companies looking to become publicly traded.

Companies can list on more than one stock exchange. For example, a company may be traded in Tokyo, but have a secondary listing in New York. A company may choose to have a secondary listing as a way of raising its profile and capital in that country.

Communicating a share offering

The communications during an initial public offering (IPO) or secondary listing or divesting of shares is of exceptional importance. IPO communications have their own set of formulaic tasks and rules. Overall, they focus on creating a positive reputation for a company before, during, and after flotation. The qualities of a company most important to investors are communicated in the financial media and investment community.

While each country in Asia has different rules, handling the communications for an IPO generally follows these basic steps:

Define the communication objectives—to generate interest among local, institutional, and retail investor audiences and, eventually, gain support for the flotation and its pricing after the announcement;

Define communication strategies—to develop a series of messages to encourage the target investors to support the flotation and its pricing—covering the strengths, growth potential, and management experience; and

Develop a communications plan—to project a positive image during the flotation and raise the profile of company spokespersons.

Activities under a typical IPO program might eventually look something like this:

Step 1 Before the financial regulatory authority has agreed to allow the company to list:

- Media releases and interviews on the business development of the company and industry-related issues, speaking opportunities at industry-related forums, production of company brochures and updated information on the website, and holding of media training for the company spokespeople to give them the skills required to tackle the IPO communications

Step 2 After the financial regulatory authority has agreed to allow the company to list:

- Development of the non-financial section of the investment prospective and presentation materials, media briefings and one-on-one interviews for senior management, and presentations via a road show or webcast to analysts, fund managers, and media to communicate the strength of the company

Step 3 Announcement of flotation:

- Highly proactive media relations though media conferences, media releases, and one-on-one interviews to maximize the exposure of the company during this period; print advertisements in major economic newspapers; and distribution of positive research to analysts and the media

Step 4 After flotation:

- Announcing the success of the listing with a media conference, interviews, and media releases; arrangement of a high profile listing celebration and advertisements to celebrate the success of the flotation; and preparation for first earnings release.

Case Study

The Australian Pipeline Trust (APA) was spun-off from Australian utility AGL to unlock value for AGL and allow the Australian Pipeline Trust to operate independently and with its own identity. Hugh Fraser, now of FCC Partners, led the investor relations for the IPO, managing the following activities:

- First, an audit of likely issues was conducted and used as the basis for developing a comprehensive issues kit and IPO communication plan. Then sales messages and a range of marketing material, including media releases, fact sheets, and corporate brochures were created. The leadership team also undertook presentation and media training and coaching.
- At the same time, a profile-building campaign took place to raise awareness of the CEO within the utilities industry.
- The IR team worked with lead underwriters (ABN-AMRO) and other advisers to ensure consistent and strategic communication at all stages and verify it was legally compliant. A design theme for the

(Continued)

IPO was created called "buried treasure," which was used for the prospectus and the advertising in online and print media.

- A website was created (www.buriedtreasure.com.au), which drove traffic from other general investment sites to the site.

- A media launch and Australia-wide media tour were conducted. These events also used the *buried treasure* theme, and were followed by media outreach to financial, investment, personal finance, market, and regional media. Positive media coverage was widespread and contributed to strong demand for the offer.

- A direct mail reminder was sent to everyone who had requested a prospectus reminding them that the offer was closing soon.

The issue raised over A$200 million and was comfortably oversubscribed. The case demonstrates how a well-planned and executed IPO can not only achieve a successful outcome in raising money, but also provide the basis of a strong, long-term corporate reputation.

Source: Hugh Fraser, Principal, FCC Partners.

Investor relations in mergers and acquisitions

Much of the work in investor relations is in mergers and acquisitions; disseminating the company's message, while countering the effects of the opposition's communications.

The best defense against a takeover should be the strength of the company's operation and its share price. However, in reaching this position, the defender will be working hard to demonstrate that management has good support within the company and from the company's board.

As a takeover attack develops, almost daily disclosure of information is essential to maintain the loyalty of the company's various stakeholder groups—including shareholders and analysts, as well as employees, customers, suppliers, and the media. In defending a company against a takeover, investor relations practitioners generally focus on pinpointing the deficiencies of the opposition's operation and bid, as well as focusing on the positive aspects of the defender's own company. Direct communication is made with the shareowners to dissuade them from selling and, maybe, to make them a counter offer as a way of bringing the shares into more manageable hands.

The role of the aggressor's investor relations team is very similar to that of the defense's. They need to demonstrate the credibility of the takeover bid and the hostile company's stature. The communication will focus on how the merger will benefit the shareholders, customers, suppliers, and employers. The aggressor has, of course, may have the advantage of surprise and the chance to prepare long in advance.

But, even if the proposed merger is friendly, it is important for the acquiring company and its target to establish a good relationship with community leaders and businessmen.

With a successful takeover, the victorious group needs to move quickly to ensure that key managers and employees do not leave and current suppliers and customers do not defect during the period of re-adjustment.

Some hostile mergers fail in the long run because post takeover communications have been poor—key employees have departed, important customers lost, and local communities turned against the company. Post-merger communications campaigns should be well planned to go into action as soon as the deal is done. Multilevel communication needs to continue with all of the stakeholder groups involved to prove beyond doubt the long-term benefits of the takeover.

Case Study

When Chinese Internet search engine Baidu listed on Nasdaq in 2005, it worked with Hill & Knowlton to position itself with US investors as a company with many competitive strengths.

The strategy focused on the uncertain environment for Chinese companies listing in the US, generally because of a lack of disclosure and transparency and a poor track record of other companies listing in the months prior. Thus, Baidu was positioned as the trusted market leader in China and a platform for China's burgeoning e-commerce industry. The investor relations program included developing the prospectus and implementing a media outreach program to ensure a consistent message was being delivered to media and potential investors.

Baidu's IPO was oversubscribed by 60 percent and raised US$86 million. The stock price also increased by 350 percent, the biggest first day gain of a newly-listed company since 2000.

Source: Asia Pacific PR Awards 2005.

Connecting in a crisis

Of course, the financial market is equally susceptible to crises as the consumer market. Political troubles, financial downturns, manufacturing problems, and strikes can all cause severe problems and rock confidence in the company. In recent years there has also been a growing number of scandals surrounding the fraudulent actions of company directors.

In October 2008, just five months after it had to admit the miscounting of a mere 225 million votes at its AGM to re-elect managing director, the Honorable Henry Fan Hung-ling, CITIC Pacific stunned the Hong Kong market by announcing—six weeks after the initial discovery—it had losses of US$1.99 billion, due to foreign exchange exposures.

The fallout was immediate, with trading of shares suspended. The resignations of the group finance director and group financial controller were accepted and the scandal delivered a devastating blow to executive council member and government-appointed executive director of CITIC Pacific, Henry Fan, who had to request a leave of absence from a stream of influential appointments. These included the Board of Hong Kong Exchanges and Clearing Limited (HKEx), chairmanship of the Takeovers and Mergers Panel, treasurer to The University of Hong Kong, and, critically, as a member of Hong Kong's Executive Council and the Chairman of the Mandatory Provident Fund Schemes Authority.

The media and Internet coverage continued for several months, including an ongoing tracking of the situation on the highly influential www.webb-site.com, which provides independent commentary on corporate and economic governance, business, finance, investment, and regulatory affairs in Hong Kong.

Most of the public and media could not understand how CITIC Pacific had become involved in such a risky investment in the first place and were angry at the delay in admitting the loss. The investor relations team was kept busy, issuing as many as four media release in the first two days alone. After months of being in a reactive mode, the role of the investor relations team was to rebuild CITIC Pacific's reputation and the trust of its investors. This was no easy task given that the campaign had to begin in the middle of the autumn 2008 financial crisis.

Case Study

The privatization of Indonesian Bank Mandiri in 2002 was especially challenging against a background of an economic downturn, increased terrorism, and the Iraq war. Resistance was high because stakeholders believed the privatization was taking place at the direction of the IMF.

An investor audit was conducted among the investment community, media, and legislative stakeholders in Jakarta, Singapore, and Hong Kong. On the basis of the audit, Bank Mandiri's communications focused on communicating the bank's turnaround and its stock as a "must-own" investment for Southeast Asia-facing institutions.

Prior to the IPO, Bank Mandiri began holding quarterly analyst and media briefings. A case study was developed by business school INSEAD to demonstrate the transformation of the bank. The IPO was 6.7 times oversubscribed and raised US$320 million.

Source: Asia Pacific PR Awards 2003.

Government economic plans

But it's not just companies that face communication issues—on a larger scale, governments are constantly utilizing financial public relations to attract foreign investment and maintain confidence in their monetary systems. A well-documented case is the global program for Korea's Ministry of Finance and Economy in the midst of the 1997 financial crisis, as it worked with the IMF to develop and implement a drastic economic reform plan. The Korean government had not been in the habit of needing to communicate, but it had to take charge of the global dialogue and communicate strategies to an international audience.

As a result of effective communication, the macro economy stabilized more quickly than any other country in East Asia.

Growth of financial services

Before we leave this section, we should not forget the communication opportunities in the financial services sector. The term financial public relations is the generic one covering all aspects of strategic communication engaging those who invest in companies and their product or people who impact the decisions underlying investments. Banks, credit card and consumer finance companies, hedge funds, mutual funds, brokerages, insurance companies, and venture capital and private equity firms all require financial public relations to help sell products and services, such as insurance policies, mutual funds, mortgages, and online brokers. Activities might include development of brochures and other collateral material, media relations, speaking engagements, and other activities designed to strengthen relationships with financial intermediaries such as conferences, factory visits, and internal communications.

The investor relations specialist needs both communication and financial skills. While being a good communicator, as in any area of public relations work, they also need to have a good specialist understanding of finance and accounting issues. Keeping on top of changing regulatory environments is a major challenge, as is striving to make the best use of new technology.

Effective shareholder communication is an indispensable part of any corporate strategy. Companies that get it right can reap huge financial and reputational rewards. And CEOs who understand the importance of shareholder communication—remembering who the real owners are of a listed company—will always come out on top in the long run whatever the financial climate.

Treating the Communications Patient

Healthcare public relations

Health is an issue at the top of personal, media, and government agendas these days as we become more educated and have more access to information via the Internet, which has led to a boom in "self-care." Mindful of these trends, governments in Asia Pacific and globally realize that, in addition to healthcare product manufacturers and service providers, they have to engage more fully with their populations on this complex subject to regulate and manage the relationship between patient and doctor, and between customers and medical products and services. These trends are making healthcare into one of the fastest growing niche public relations areas in Asia providing significant public relations opportunities.

Healthcare in Asia Pacific

Populations throughout most Southeast Asian countries are highly sensitized to healthcare issues as when the specter of avian flu became a reality in the winter season of 1998 onward causing annual deaths in Vietnam, China, Hong Kong, and Indonesia across all demographic groupings of the population. This was closely followed by the SARS outbreak in 2003, which spread outward from China, via Hong Kong to Taiwan and Toronto.

The exponential growth in Asia's indigenous populations alongside the increase in personal wealth is also stimulating turnover of the healthcare sector in Asia.

In terms of pharmaceutical and healthcare industries, China and India are heading up the business growth in Asia, with talk of 50 percent growth common and market forecasts for the Indian pharmaceutical industry projected at five times their current values from US$5 billion to US$25 billion by 2010. Meanwhile, China is tipped to be the world's leader in pharmaceutical production by 2020. Already among the top ten producers of drugs, its market is estimated to be growing at 27.7 percent annually, compared to the US at 7 percent.[1]

Other issues complicate the provision of healthcare in Asia Pacific. In the public sector, governments with tighter budgets have to manage their healthcare more efficiently, with doctors alone being pressurized to work longer hours and required to deliver better services on less money. Medical care is a high cost item on the agenda for most governments and new technological advances in diagnosis only add to these costs. Increasingly, populations across Asia Pacific are being encouraged to assume more responsibility for their own healthcare though private medicine and insurance.

Also, issues management and public affairs input is needed to ensure quality control in the pharmaceutical production industry as counterfeit drugs, parallel imports, and fast-tracked drugs are being launched in the market before the existing authentic brands and this requires some form of public relations management.

Case Study

Chronic obstructive pulmonary disease (COPD) is Australia's fourth biggest killer, yet few are familiar with the term. In 2005, The Australian Lung Foundation (ALF), therefore, commissioned Burson-Marsteller to raise awareness of World COPD Day (November 16).

The target was to reach undiagnosed women and men, GPs (general practitioners), ALF sponsors, and government committee members on health. Burson-Marsteller was tasked to reach three million Australians, to substantially increase the number of ALF COPD support groups, and to expand ALF's political contacts.

The consultancy commissioned new research demonstrating the need for improved community awareness, set out to motivate local evangelists, and used patient case studies to bring COPD to life and demonstrate the benefit of an early diagnosis.

Important new data was utilized to show that one in six Australians above the age of 45 had some form of COPD, but three-quarters of them were unaware of it. A particular focus was on women with COPD.

Journalists throughout Australia were given localized media alerts and video new releases were sent to TV journalists featuring interviews and background as well as general media kits. William Darbishire, ALF CEO said the campaign was the most successful PR campaign ever undertaken by ALF.

The campaign reached seven million consumers; calls to the ALF helpline increased 100 percent during the campaign month; and the ALF was invited by the government to appear before the Backbench Committee on Health and Aging.

Source: Burson-Marsteller Australia and The Australian Lung Foundation.

Cultural and local dimensions of healthcare

The first information that people in Hong Kong received about the SARS outbreak was in the form of anecdotal news stories in local newspapers about the unusual shortage and a run on vinegar in Southern China across the border in January 2003. At the time nobody thought anything of it—food scares or panic-buying often happen in line with fluctuating commodity values.

Yet, precisely at this juncture it would have been wise for the Hong Kong government and medical specialists, in addition to the community at-large, to pay attention to this story and question why this was happening. When young, healthy people and children among others began to fall gravely ill and were hospitalized in February and March with an unknown pneumonia-like illness, the questions almost came too late.

It seemed that the answers lay in the fact that this severe flu-like illness had been affecting large numbers of the population in Southern China since October 2002. It had a significant mortality rate and the traditional flu cure of hot vinegar was the popular remedy being dispensed in homes across the region, which caused the much reported vinegar shortage as people realized the severity of the disease and essentially took matters in their own hands.

Of course, there was no patented cure—Tamiflu had not been invented yet, and this story shows how in Asia, home-grown medical remedies and cures are to be respected. On another level, we can see how the lack of any knowledge or information about the disease led to self remedy, which also has public relations implications in terms of the need to educate audiences in more effective healthcare options. This case is also a good example of effective crisis communications management which we cover in chapter 8.

In Asia Pacific, modern healthcare practices co-exist alongside traditional forms of remedies, such as the use of vinegar as an antibiotic, and this synergy appears to work well. For healthcare public relations initiatives in Asia, this local cultural dimension creates both challenges and opportunities as local sensitivities and needs, plus contingent legal ramifications, must always be factored into the healthcare dialogue.

Patient empowerment

The cultural landscape of healthcare is altering in relation to the changes that are being witnessed in patient behavior. Traditionally, in Asian communities, patients have looked to their family or immediate community to discuss healthcare problems or seek more information about illness. But a 2006 survey of patients conducted by Weber Shandwick in Asian markets, including China, Hong Kong, Singapore, South Korea, and Taiwan, found that although the doctor is perceived to be the main source of medical information for those on prescription drugs, a significant amount of people are turning to the Internet to check out their symptoms prior to their appointment and after to check out the diagnosis.

From the 817 patients surveyed, all of who had chronic illnesses such as asthma, hepatitis B, or diabetes, it was found that over 75 percent of them had consulted the Internet prior to their medical appointments. In addition, half of them (55 percent) had talked about their findings with their doctors, with 37 percent of them asking for specific brands of prescription drugs, resulting in 64 percent of these patients being prescribed the requested brands.

This is a significant shift in attitudes and related behaviors among Asian medical consumers who appear to be bypassing the traditional Confucian respect for professional authority by taking matters into their own hands to self-prescribe and self-validate the diagnosis and prescribed treatment.

From the public relations perspective, this patient empowerment trend suggests that the Internet and news media carrying medical stories are being recognized as valued sources of medical information for diagnostic and treatment purposes. Certainly since the emergence of SARS and avian flu as pandemic possibilities, medical stories have been higher on the media agenda in Asia Pacific and around the world. This is also supplemented by a global interest in improving the quality of life, increasing longevity, and personal health management with widespread resulting media coverage of these issues in daily newspapers and magazines. Again this is validated by the survey, which found that over 50 percent of respondents claimed to feel more confident about taking medication when they had read about it in a media source and were also more likely to continue with this medication as a consequence.

Public relations approaches to healthcare

This is a complex and rapidly developing field focusing on the ongoing effort to raise awareness among healthcare professionals about new medical breakthroughs and health policies, while also educating citizens about health issues and ensuring that consumers are attracted to the point-of-sale for new healthcare products and services.

As most countries in Asia Pacific restrict the advertising of prescription drugs, public relations activities are an ideal and viable way of getting the message across to consumers about new medical developments. More than in any other sector, consumers are fascinated by healthcare news and feature stories to determine how healthcare and health related issues will directly impact them. Every day newspapers and Internet news sites in Asia Pacific carry medical stories covered by a team of healthcare reporters always on the look out for breaking news on health issues.

The critical role from a PR perspective is managing the push of information from producer to healthcare practitioners and the push of information to healthcare consumers. The winning situation would be where the healthcare professionals would be the first to receive timely information about a new drug before it was released to wider stakeholder groups via the Internet and the print/broadcast media. But this is not replicated in reality, leaving many healthcare professionals frustrated at being out of the information loop—which doctors would relish their patients being more knowledgeable about a new monitoring mechanism for diabetes than they were? Equally, public relations professionals must keep themselves ahead of the game and constantly be up-to-date about medical developments, as healthcare reporters have daily access to breaking medical news on the Internet.

HEALTHCARE STAKEHOLDERS

Public relations healthcare specialists will engage with a range of professional medical audiences:

- General practitioners
- Pharmacists
- Doctors
- Nurses
- Hospital administrators
- Government departments
- Health insurance firms
- Medical reporters

Public relations professionals' involvement in healthcare usually concerns the following areas:

Ethical   Ethical healthcare or prescription-only products require a strategic marketing approach as the message about the new drug must be delivered in a timely way to the key audiences mindful of the local legal and regulatory framework. In most countries across Asia Pacific, prescription-only drugs cannot be advertised by brand name in any form of promotional materials such as an advert or news release. Given this constraint, the public relations healthcare practitioner acts as the link between the journalists and the pharmaceutical spokesperson to facilitate effective and responsible media coverage.

Over-the-Counter (OTC) products dispensed without prescription   By way of contrast, the public relations professional has to manage the brand profile of OTC medical products such as headache tablets and ear drops to keep them visible both with activity action aimed at pharmacists and also in consumer media channels. Although many of these products may have been on the pharmacy shelves for a long time—or enjoyed a precious life as a prescription-only drug—the news angle must be based on providing informed and balanced information from a credible source, whether that is a medical expert or a consumer opinion poll.

Community education programs   Using educational, awareness-raising campaigns to promote awareness of a medical issue or condition is a credible way of getting the healthcare message across to a wide range of stakeholders. The news angle is critical here as the health reporters will be looking for a good news hook, such as new research findings on the cure for a disease or the actual number of people likely to be affected by a disease in the future and the related health costs to the tax payer.

Hospital promotion   While people like to feel reassured that they have access to local, qualified medical professionals in the public and private sectors—many people in certain cultures are uncertain about hospitals, and others are critical of their services. So the hospitals' stories about their services and staff need to be told in a positive and professional way, using communication vehicles including information leaflets, charitable fundraisers, and open day events, where the hospitals invite the local community to visit and view their services.

Digital communication   There are many local and global websites in a range of languages devoted to health issues, diagnosis, and prescription on the Internet such as www.medicalsymptomsonline.com or online medical journal sites, such as the Asia Pacific Association of Medical Toxology at www.asiatox.org, which now holds, recently published medical journals.

While this is an indicator of immense interest in the subject and the growth in self-management of health, it places huge pressure on PR healthcare professionals to deliver the most up-to-date information to medical specialists before it is posted on the Internet and accessed by consumers or journalists.

Techniques for Healthcare Public Relations

Given the restrictions placed on healthcare promotion, the following activities have an educational slant to get the message across about the medical product or service without using the brand name, but by awareness-raising in terms of association with the organization producing them.

Public opinion surveys: These can be angled in various ways around the product or issue to be newsworthy—by promoting a fast acting painkiller where you could survey the number of times that people had headaches in a month for example.

Sponsored events: Companies can sponsor or tie into special events targeted to the specific audiences, for example, children's fun days by vaccination companies or sports events for muscle treatment or physiological services.

Sponsored leaflets about a disease and its management: Information leaflets for display in medical centers, hospital waiting rooms, and doctors' clinics can be produced by healthcare and pharmaceutical companies focusing on a specific disease, its cause, symptoms, prevention, or treatment and longer-term prognosis. Companies producing folic acid tablets needed for the growth of healthy fetuses target pregnant women in this way for example.

Media relations: Generating news and feature-style stories lies at the heart of the public relations healthcare effort. These stories can appear as news of a healthcare breakthrough or editorial coverage by a medical expert on a specific disease and its remedy or prevention. This could be an article in a parenting magazine on the benefits of vaccinations for children with a timeline illustrating when each vaccine should be dispensed throughout childhood.

Practitioner seminars: Pharmaceutical companies often sponsor workshops or seminars for medical practitioners—doctors and nurses—about

(Continued)

a specific disease or condition. It is also a good way of generating a database of interested medical specialists in the area of health being addressed.

Special interest meetings: These are seminars with a wider, non-specialist stakeholder group interested in a particular medical condition. At this type of event, a new drug can be launched by a medical specialist and the media invited to cover the story.

Community outreach programs: Typically these are visits by a healthcare expert to schools or community centers to raise awareness about a medical condition such as TB or an STD and how it can be avoided, detected, and cured. Here, the disease or condition is carefully aligned with the target audience as part of their social education program.

Digital communication: Developing and updating website content for the pharmaceutical or healthcare organization is a good way of gaining visibility for the producer and their products and services. It enables the public relations healthcare professional to disseminate healthcare information and engage with stakeholders in a creative way using medical blogs on medical issues and topics for example.

Crafting a healthcare media story

Most people have an insatiable curiosity about health, especially if it relates to them now or in the future. Look at daily newspapers across Asia Pacific to prove this point, as a medical story about malpractice in Hong Kong, the latest findings about rising diabetes in Japan, or a health–related story about a new drug to boost longevity in Vietnam will appear in the news and features sections respectively. Here are some media tactics to boost your chances of getting medical or healthcare journalists to cover your health-care story:

- **Keep it simple:** Health issues and medical information are usually highly complex and full of detailed jargon. The PR effort must be angled to simplify the story ensuring that spokespersons are well prepared with key messages that will be understood by the health reporter (and their relative medical knowledge) in addition to the average consumer with very little medical understanding.

Case Study

If you are squeamish, you may want to miss this case study... Genital warts are hardly at the top of the conversational agenda in households across Taiwan, and this ensured that 3M Taiwan's Aldara cream was all the more memorable.

The Aldara launch relied almost exclusively on public relations, because of the ban on prescription medicine advertising in Taiwan, so 3M realized the critical need to educate "hidden" patients by providing research and information that was hitherto unavailable. As 30 percent of genital warts patients are below the age of 20, a campaign targeting youth was devised to deal with the two main barriers to young people addressing the subject, namely embarrassment and ignorance.

A program was developed based on the creation of *When Harry Met Sally* comic book characters, as well as arranging a "sex dialogue" panel discussion, and organizing a media conference in a famous Taichung nightclub, the nightlife capital of Taiwan.

The comic book characters played a major role in the campaign, serving as a communication bridge using a website and a tailor-made comic book style leaflet that connected with the popularity of this type of media among young Taiwanese.

The "sex dialogue" provided an involving and participative angle to the narrative, lining up a panel that saw healthcare experts along with a well-known celebrity known as the "Nightclub Queen" voicing their views on sex awareness that ranged from educational to street-wise. The nightclub provided a recurring motif throughout the campaign— which has relevance being the social location where the spread of STDs often starts.

The nightclub was also used as the site of the media conference. 3M was able to exceed its business objectives on a relatively low budget. Significantly, the majority of dermatologists now prescribe Aldara, and the product's fourth quarter revenue in 2003 reached parity with the annual revenue made by its main competitor. The program itself generated 198 media placements with the website receiving postings of over 1,000 messages and it also received near to one million visitors in a two-month timeline.

Source: Asia Pacific PR Awards 2004.

- **Tell the human story:** Stories that focus on the human application and impact of the drug or medical condition are highly appealing as feature-style coverage in print and broadcast media.

- **Go for the majority:** Journalists will be attracted by stories that cover diseases and their medication that affect the mass majority of the population or conditions which threaten to do so in the future. Diabetes, asthma, heart conditions, and cancer are stories that do not saturate the media as audiences are constantly seeking solutions to these medical problems both personally and in relation to loved ones.

- **Choose your mouthpiece carefully:** Be strategic about the choice of a medical or healthcare spokesperson. Being an eminent doctor provides a credible platform but he or she must be able to communicate the message in a clear and informative way to the journalist and the consumer.

- **Keep it local:** This traditional news value applies to healthcare PR as in all other aspects of the job when it comes to generating stories in the media, so find a local angle to a global story and a local spokesperson or patient to validate the narrative as it will generate more interest and be less remote to the audience.

- **Be visual:** Healthcare products and services are ideal for show-and-tell approaches—a scientific drawing demonstrating a new hearing aid breakthrough, a cartoon showing which part of the body a new drug targets, or a photo of people being administered the latest anti-flu vaccine are all compelling ways to tell the healthcare story.

- **Try to make the unfashionable appear exceptional:** Some medical conditions are not as "trendy" or approachable as others because they are so routine, such as headaches, or have a cultural taboo attached to them, such as impotence. But if the news angle and hook are worked on—localize it, humanize it, apply it to many—then the news value increases significantly.

- **Tie it up with a ribbon:** Healthcare news stories submitted to journalists as a neat package with all news angles covered, are likely to be attractive as you are thinking like a journalist and positioning your story from their point of need.

Putting It into Practice

- *Media Expert*: Dr. Tong, Surgical team leader in Hong Kong
- *Patient suffering from condition*: Mr. Wong, 56 year old businessman first to receive new hearing implant "*I can now hear most sounds and whispering for the first time.*"
- *News angle*: New hearing implant placed in inner ear recovers 90 percent of patient's hearing range, likened to a cripple throwing away their crutch
- *Result*: 5,000–10,000 severely deaf patients with previously unsuccessful traditional implants will now be able to hear again
- *Visuals*: Illustration of where implant is placed and photo of the magnetic implant charger that is placed on skin
- *Factoid*: Over 800,000 people in Hong Kong suffer from severe hearing impairment

Source: Adapted from *South China Morning Post*, November 26, 2008, City Section, C1.

Strategies for engagement with healthcare professionals

While healthcare public relations is increasingly focused on the pull to stimulate consumer demand for branded medicines, the push to have healthcare professionals engaged in healthcare products and services is equally important. Healthcare communication efforts also focus on direct engagement with healthcare professionals through sponsorship of conference events, invitations to healthcare equipment demonstrations, and the provision of collateral materials.

Case Study

In Hong Kong, one woman dies every day from cervical cancer. Until recently, there has been little women could do to protect themselves against this cancer. Instead, the focus has been on early detection through regular Pap screening.

With Cervarix, a new cervical cancer vaccine that provides 100 percent protection against the most common cancer-causing viruses HPV 16 and 18, this picture was set to change. GlaxoSmithKline Hong Kong challenged Weber Shandwick to launch Cervarix in Q1 2008. The launch had to encourage women, who had some awareness of cervical cancer, to

(Continued)

seek vaccination against HPV 16 and 18, and continue with regular Pap screening.

Weber Shandwick created a multilayered and emotionally-engaging launch campaign to achieve this with a dual branded and non-branded focus. An emotional call to action, "Shall we talk? Act now!" was created to drive the unbranded campaign, with the branded campaign based on clinical data for Cervarix. Building emotion into the campaign was essential, as women are already aware of this cancer, but need an added impetus to seek vaccination. "Shall we talk? Act now!" encouraged women to share information from the launch campaign and created a personal connection with this health risk issue by encouraging women to get a vaccination for themselves as well as their daughters, sisters, and friends.

Weber Shandwick created messages, and visual synergy between print and outdoor advertising and a multilayered launch campaign which included media relations, direct marketing, celebrity endorsement, community outreach, web-based information, primary care physician endorsement, and a first-of-its-kind alliance of doctors committed to improving women's understanding of cervical cancer and the need for vaccination.

The product launch included presentations from key female health specialists and a heartfelt testimonial from a local female celebrity, bridging the branded and non-branded campaigns. This was followed by a fashion show with celebrities modeling the unbranded awareness message, "Shall we talk? Act now!" emblazoned on one-off T-shirt designs created by a local celebrity fashion designer and amplified through mass designs created by local design students.

Post-launch the team worked with an international fashion photographer to create a unique photo book, which captured the emotional bond between mothers and their daughters in impactful imagery and heartfelt mother-daughter messages. Weber Shandwick also took the "Shall we talk? Act now!" message to the local community with an educational shopping-center road show and launched the Cervical Cancer Prevention Alliance (CCPA) of doctors committed to improving cervical cancer awareness in Hong Kong.

The emotional and rational connection of this special campaign was augmented by the creation of "Shall we talk? Act now!" advocates in the form of celebrities, a fashion designer, physicians, and Hong Kong mothers and daughters. These advocates helped secure a connection with Hong Kong women to break down the barriers to talking about this disease and for every woman to act now to seek vaccination.

Source: Weber Shandwick Hong Kong.

Turning Technospeak into Everyday Talk

Asia Pacific is the fastest growing geography for technology public relations, as each side of the digital divide draws ever closer. There is no doubt that technology itself continually advances, fueled by innovation and the global trend-bucking growth of chip sales in China and India to, literally, the all-singing and all-dancing wireless devices of Korea and Japan. Industry professionals working with wireless telecommunications will attest to the fact that counties such as Korea and Japan were light years ahead of the rest of the world when it came to mobile phones. Wireless devices powered by 3G technology burst into our consciousness in the late 1990s, while the world could only look on in envy as Korean and Japanese consumers downloaded games, took photographs, and even used their phones for karaoke.

Good technology needs good public relations. There is no doubt that great technologies can be so irresistible, they sell themselves. However, like every other aspect of public relations, it is a case of putting the technology in the right hands in the first place.

But what do we mean by technology when it comes to public relations? At its broadest definition, it could be defined as any product or service which utilizes science in a practical way. When we think of technology, however, we generally categorize it as covering computers, software, and telecommunications. While electrical and white goods such as TVs and washing machines also utilize the same level of technology, we deal with them in the sphere of marketing communications.

Similar to financial and healthcare communications, technology public relations is made up of several sub-specialties, including semi-conductors, business software, PCs, and wireless technology.

More than 10 years ago, author Mary Devereux said that technology communications had escaped the bindings of business communications to become a practice area on its own.[2] There was, however, a point in 1999 and 2000, after the bursting of the dotcom bubble, when the technology practice looked to be in danger of being folded back into business marketing. At that time, we were looking at digital communications as the focus of campaigns. With digital now moving into its rightful place as a communication vehicle, technology public relations has maintained its status as an individual specialty.

Point of View

"Technology is an increasingly integral part of our lives—both at work and play. From 3G smartphones that offer superior e-mailing and Internet experiences, to the latest GPS restaurant finder services, it is clear that technology PR professionals will have to address an even wider stakeholder base than before.

At Qualcomm, we believe in a holistic approach to communications planning to ensure that such opportunities are addressed; that we maintain dialogue to regulatory stakeholders as much as business media outlets and lifestyle/entertainment publications. It is through such an approach that the stories of technology companies will be made aware of and, more importantly, understood in the appropriate context."

Adrian Fu, Manager, Public Relations, Southeast Asia & Pacific, Qualcomm International

---

It's about the technology

It stands to reason that if you are promoting the latest in technology, you should be employing the latest technology to do so. There is a, maybe apocryphal, tale that in the late 90s, IBM Hong Kong invited presentations from public relations consultancies and refused to let one firm present when they began to use overhead transparencies. Many of us may also remember a wonderful story that circulated about the launch of Microsoft's Windows 95 software, also in Hong Kong, when the audience was not only surprised to witness a dance show but laughed out loud when one of the dancers held her letter "W" upside down.

This is why, in recent years, several firms have actively engaged with digital technology to reach their audiences. Many firms work with bloggers to demonstrate their products and evoke a reaction online. Several IT conferences these days have "blogger corners" where influential bloggers are invited to participate in the conference and report directly on their blogs in real time.

Techno-messages

Technology practitioners need to address widely different audiences, from consumers and analysts to the huge army of engineers and developers. They also need to be able to talk to CIOs and IT managers within vendors, customers, consultants, investors, media, analysts, legislators, and regulators.

However, when it comes down to the basics, it is all about communicating a benefit. This is why a key talent of any public relations professional is the ability to translate "techno speak" into a language that the audience can understand; reducing the jargon to the minimum and clearly differentiating the messages.

Like most other specialties, technology public relations draws from a broad range of expertise, including media relations, consumer and business marketing, public affairs, and corporate reputation. This is why, in addition to media relations, the typical technology campaign would include a variety of activities, including media relations, advocacy, and user-group communications.

In any technology campaign, there will be a large element of education; helping the target audience understand how to use the technology and, more importantly, understand its benefits. Demonstrations and product loans are a traditional method of engaging the media; allowing the media a hands-on experience is a valuable way of showing them its benefits.

Advocacy groups

There may be times when a message being communicated, however well-delivered and supported, will not be accepted by the public simply because of the messenger. The creation of advocacy groups can help technology companies take part in public debate and government hearings as part of an industry effort. These groups often lobby governments and regulators to legislate in the corporate interest; such as allowing more licensing. Good examples are the Asian arms of the two 3G wireless industry groups, the CDMA Development Group, which promotes the adoption of CDMA technology, and the GSM Association, which advocates the rival technology. Over the years, the two groups have fought it out in the media, at conferences, and with industry analysts.

Industry analysts

Analyst programs are core to most technology campaigns. Industry analysts provide their own clients with advice on their IT and product

Case Study

Continuing the wireless phone theme, Qualcomm, a leader in 3G technologies, wanted to drive its Asia Pacific leadership in 3G mobile communications. It worked with Burson-Marsteller to "evangelize" its technology, which is driving the adoption of 3G mobile services. It aimed to highlight economic benefits of 3G services in the growing markets of Southeast Asia, including Hong Kong, India, Indonesia, Malaysia, Singapore, Taiwan, Thailand, Vietnam, and Cambodia; provide tangible support to the firm's business expansion in Europe and Latin America by showcasing the impact of CDMA and 3G in Asia; and demonstrate to handset manufacturers, service providers, and application developers in all markets, the revenue and new business potential enabled by partnering with Qualcomm.

The program strategy was based on a three-pronged approach:

- "Hero Partners": Promote business partners to speak on behalf of 3G to the media and at industry forums
- "Real and Relevant Media Program": Take advantage of cross-market interest in 3G innovation and expanding media appeal by moving the story from technology to lifestyle applications
- "Thought Leadership & Advocacy": Target direct to analysts and industry groups, with road shows, meetings, and white papers

The campaign reached virtually every relevant broadcaster and publication in the region—from India to Australia and New Zealand—both at their home bases and via correspondents in key Qualcomm markets, including Asian correspondents based throughout the world. In all, Qualcomm interacted with more than 650 media contacts during 2003, creating overall awareness of its issues and achieving more than 3,000 media results across the region. Features, VNRs (video news releases), and media contacts generated in Asia have also been a major driver of Qualcomm coverage in the vital markets of the US, Europe, and Latin America.

Source: Qualcomm.

strategy—and they have become a powerful influencer of customers and the media. There are thousands of analysts around the world, and all the major firms are well represented in Asia Pacific, including Gartner Group, Forrester Research, and IDC.

Each industry analyst specializes in his/her own area and many of them are famous figures in their own right. Talking with analysts is not like talking with the media however. Analysts have an insatiable appetite for data and can absorb far more complex material than the average journalist, even if they do specialize in technology.

Most public relations professionals will attest to the fact that analyst relations can be a great deal more pleasurable than media relations, on a good day. After all, it is the analysts' job to gather information and engage with technology companies, in order that they can give the very best advice and recommendations to their own clients. And, of course, there is always the element that analysts will want to sell you services and consulting.

Dealing with IT analysts, however, requires that public relations professionals match their level of expertise with the analysts, as far as possible, and understand what the analyst requires in terms of useful information. The public relations professional will also have to, as in other specialist areas such as healthcare and financial PR, repackage the information to reach more diverse audiences beyond a straightforward business-to-business focus. As IT now underpins most of the operational functions of organizations, wider stakeholders need to be engaged beyond the IT vendor and the specialist publications they read. We also need to look at finance directors and members of the procurement committee. This wider stakeholder focus may include more mainstream

Case Study

Global technology company NCR Corporation was importing its FastLane self-checkout technology to Australia from the US and Europe in 2002. It was a difficult task, as the media were convincing readers that introducing high-tech retailing would result in job losses; this was not the case.

NCR partnered with the Australian Retailers Association at the Retail Business Technology Exhibition in September 2002, to showcase the technology to the media and retailers. Constructive dialogue helped NCR educate the media on the benefits of the technology and clearly explain the company's position. This resulted in more impartial or positive media coverage.

Source: Asia Pacific PR Awards 2003.

media involvement, in addition to the trade media promoting messages that focus on the benefits rather than purely the technological features.

Road shows, conferences, and exhibitions

Asia hosts some of the world's largest and most influential IT industry conferences and exhibitions. Most major firms will have a presence at these events, be they exhibitors, speakers, or hosting an off-site event. Semicon is one of the most well-known trade shows, which organizes events all around the world.

Companies also frequently develop programs to engage directly with software developers, whom they hope will adopt their technologies as the base platform for their programs. For example, Intel hosts the Intel Developer Forum, gathering engineers and developers to discuss Intel products and products based around Intel technology. The growing importance of Asia was highlighted when Intel held its first IDF outside of the US in Beijing in 2007 and when San Francisco and Taipei shared the IDF events in September and October 2008.

Case Study

Until 2004 LG had been considered a second-tier mobile phone manufacturer as consumers lacked confidence in its product quality. Since then, LG has developed a new concept of a premium handset series, the LG Black Label Series (BLS), in efforts to differentiate it from its competitors.

LG's BLS is a premium mobile handset series that features cutting edge technology as well as superior design. LG has launched three products on the name of LG BLS and each handset has its own distinctive design and technology; LG Chocolate's sleek and glossy look with the world's first touch keypad, LG Shine's shining full metal body, and LG Secret's long-lasting style with innovative materials. These different style handsets represent the sensuality and style that today's consumers are demanding from their phones.

LG BLS approached consumers using emotional marketing tactics because it realized that an emotional connection with consumers, once gained, is the most difficult thing for competitors to compete against. The below examples show how LG conducted its marketing communication activities to strengthen its relationship with consumers.   *(Continued)*

LG developed its own user-interactive communication channel in the online community. It included the company's first official blog as well as individual product blogs for its Chocolate and Shine models in several countries. In the blog, LG has not only provided news and up-to-date information on the company and its products but also hosted a number of different online competitions such as its online user created content (UCC) competition under Shine's product concept "Born to Shine."

LG launched a consumer trial event for LG Secret starting in Thailand and extending around the rest of the world. This event offered consumers an exciting opportunity to learn and experience the secret features of the phone. The events have succeeded to increase consumers' friendliness toward the BLS.

While most mobile companies focus much more on developing the technological aspects of their products, LG's BLS has taken a further step to add greater value by focusing on stylish designs and smart technology. As a result, LG's mobile phones have become cultural icons in their own right beyond enhancing quality and convenience, particularly among young consumers drawn to the innovative, the cool, and the trendy. The result has been strong sales of LG BLS products totaling 30 million units as of November 2008.

Source: Burson-Marsteller Korea and LG.

The future of technology communications looks bright; with public relations professionals ever challenged to keep pace with new developments and with the changing landscape of widening IT-focused stakeholders. Technology firms know they need to build new relationships beyond their traditional group of customers and suppliers beyond the business-to-business brief, and on the back of more creative service approaches and digital media platforms, so they can broaden their business into new markets and countries, while they hold off the competition and enhance the company's overall brand value.

Endnotes

1. Bowman, J., "Talent Crunch," *Media Magazine*, November 18, 2005, p. 10.
2. Devereux, M., *Asian PR Handbook* (Hong Kong: Hong Kong, Media & Marketing, 1997).

CHAPTER 12

The Digital Generation

Fewer subjects have received more hype in the past few years than the Internet. Everyday we are inundated with more statistics and data, which continue to surprise and excite. Now, more than 1.5 billion people have access to the Internet, and the number is growing at an annual rate of over 330 percent (Usage and World Population Statistics as of December 31, 2008).

- There are 650 million Internet users in Asia, and the size of this market is growing at an annual rate of 460 percent per year. China accounts for more than a third of these users (Internet Usage and World Population Statistics as of December 31, 2008).
- Since 2002, 133 million blogs have been indexed, and 900,000 blogs posted daily (State of the Blogosphere, September 2008, Technorati).
- People are watching hundreds of millions of videos a day on YouTube — ten hours of video is uploaded to YouTube each minute (YouTube, February 2009).
- Facebook surpassed rival MySpace in May 2008 in terms of both unique visitors and page views. Facebook welcomed 123.9 million unique visitors compared to MySpace's 114.6 and had 50.6 billion page views compared to MySpace's 45.4 billion (comScore).
- By mid 2008, Chinese language search engine Baidu ranked #3 in worldwide search market share, behind Google and Yahoo! (comScore, June 2008).
- More than half of Asia-Pacific Internet users visited online gaming sites in August 2008 (comScore, October 2008).
- Over 60 percent of the world's population will have a mobile phone by 2009, with the number of mobile subscribers passing 4 billion. (International Telecommunication Union, September 25, 2008).

What impact does the digital revolution have on the public relations industry in Asia?

When the term "media" first came into common usage, it referred to the role that newspapers played within society. It was their job to "mediate," that is frame the issues of the day and provide citizens with the information they felt was needed in a one-way flow of information.

During the 20th century, radio, television and film ushered in a new era of communications, popularly referred to as mass media, and toward the end of the 20th century, the Internet began to fuel another change in communications, opening up access to banks of knowledge previously controlled by educational and governmental institutions.

Emerging information and communication technologies began to blur the lines between production, distribution, and consumption of media content—reducing the need for mediators.

Unlike the lava lamp, digital communication is not a fad. Digital media has brought about a seismic shift in the way that corporations, governments, and any other organizations connect and converse with their stakeholders; and it is here to stay. In the old world, organizations were able to maintain a degree of control over what information they released and when. The digital phenomenon means that we live in a world where an individual can decide not only what they want to know, but also when and where they want it. They can also compare and share information with millions of other people, yet can filter out anything they deem undesirable or irrelevant.

Naturally, this digital media revolution is having a major impact on the public relations profession. As communicators of credible information, public relations professionals need to understand how they can utilize the new tools available to them to create greater relevance to their organizational or personal communication needs. It provides another communications avenue to get the message out about an organization and target a highly segmented stakeholder group.

Corporations and governments need to find entry points to talk to their audiences—and they will not be allowed access unless they are prepared to engage on appropriate and acceptable terms. Most significantly, these conversations need to be authentic, credible, and relevant.

This is nothing new for the public relations profession. We have long been in the business of engaging with key opinion leaders and the media.

The difference now is that these two groups are not limited to just a few high-level influencers. It is a common saying that everyone is now a journalist. Activists can campaign from their armchairs and even the smallest voice has a chance to be heard. Today's mediators can be literally everyone with a computer or a mobile device. They are often customers—but customers are also critics, advocates, and e-marketers through word of mouse or mobile phone.

The digital conversation is, of course, happening all over the world, but Asia is rapidly coming to the forefront of the information exchange and has the most to benefit. This is because the new PR conversations present tremendous opportunities for the region where scale and distance are an issue. Companies have long toiled with the complexity of establishing their brand and distribution channels in complex markets such as China and India. It is still early days, but access to the hinterlands of Asia—the second and third tier cities with hundreds of millions of potential customers—are gradually becoming easier as the high uptake of new communication technology in the region has effectively shrunk many of these logistical labyrinths and has brought us all closer together as more and more people get online or go mobile, and join conversations.

This presents a new challenge for the public relations industry in Asia Pacific.

Organizations expect PR professionals to understand the principles and practices as they apply directly to our profession—how journalists are using the Internet to research stories; which resources they find useful and why; which stakeholders are accessing the Internet and which locations they are visiting; how to identify, track, and work with key bloggers and online influencers; how to use the Internet to contain issues, manage crises, and talk to employees and other stakeholders; how to build and sustain brands and corporate reputations; the "hows" and "whys" of news moving between online and offline; and the potential and actual impact in all mediums.

In this chapter, we will look at some of the most important ways the public relations profession is utilizing the digital evolution.

Everyone's a Hack

With each new event on the world stage, eyewitnesses are becoming more important players, capturing the events as they happen with camera phones

---

Point of View

"The emerging new communications landscape in Asia Pacific is shaped by many factors beyond the growing Internet penetration and user generated content that are empowering individuals and providing immediate, interactive alternatives to mainstream media. Increasing freedom of speech, deregulation, and heightened competition are as or more important. There's little patience for canned corporate messages in this environment. Companies must join the conversation and have a meaningful point of view about the changing environment in which they do business if they are to earn any profile or credibility."

David Ketchum, CEO, Upstream Asia

---

and mobile digital devices. Most major networks, such as CNN, Hong Kong's TVB, and Korea's KBS have pages on their websites which allow the public to send in their photos and video, which may also be featured on live broadcast programs. Hand in hand we are also seeing the gradual dismantling of the old "press club" order which exists in some countries, such as Japan and Korea, as they bow the inevitable loss of power.

Social Media

It would be hard to find a PR professional or student who is not aware of the basic tools of the Internet these days. We are all familiar with corporate websites, which feature online media rooms, with media releases, backgrounders, webcasts, news coverage, and investor relations information. Increasingly, the Internet edition of traditional media outlets is considered just as important as the print version—maybe even better. Extranets and intranets, too, are familiar territory, providing external and internal communication for invited groups and individuals. And, of course, we are all aware of the huge research resources now available at our fingertips.

However, the real excitement for the public relations profession is the rise of social media; participatory online media where news, photos, videos, and podcasts are made public via social media websites through submission. The social media movement has spawned a whole new generation of communication methods which continue to evolve and grow on a daily basis. As it evolves, we can recognize three underlying themes:

Social media offers more opportunities for dialogue. Organizations can now communicate their message or distribute their content and enable users to provide immediate feedback, encouraging a process of dialogue between user and organization.

Social media is "stickier" than traditional media. It has high visibility and the potential to attract and hold the attention of a vast demographic of people who are now fatigued by more traditional forms of marketing and advertising. This is not always a benefit. Once information has been published, it is difficult to remove—you cannot delete history online.

Social media is viral. Because social media is so embedded in the Internet, it has a tremendous viral capacity to reach wide audiences in just a short amount of time. This represents both a substantial opportunity and threat for communications professionals.

Case Study

Asia's thriving community of bloggers is quickly becoming regarded as a trusted source of information, comparable to traditional media. Their growing influence spurred The Hoffman Agency (HA) to initiate a blogger outreach program on behalf of one of its clients, a global online search company. The client needed a cost-effective strategy to maximize the exposure of its products and to encourage more people to use them. Since bloggers are technology's early adopters and influencers, HA saw an opportunity to seek their help in promoting its customer's technology and product offerings.

To gain a better understanding of the blogging community, HA immersed itself in the blogosphere—participating in online discussions, reading blogs, engaging in conversations via popular Web 2.0 tools, joining blogger groups, and attending events. Eventually, they became bloggers themselves.

With the groundwork established, HA then initiated a two-way engagement between the client and key bloggers. By keeping bloggers in the loop about company news—offering product previews, organizing meetings,

(Continued)

and holding exclusive events—HA helped the client to grow its number of blogger contacts and also strengthen its relationship with them.

It was this show of commitment from both HA and the client that inspired Hong Kong's local bloggers to create a 118-strong Web community dedicated purely to discussing topics about the online search company.

The bloggers not only provided valuable feedback on products, but also served as evangelists for the company's applications and were often on hand to help out as user spokespeople for traditional media interviews.

In Taiwan, for instance, HA partnered with the Programmer Club—the most popular and credible online forum for programmers on the island—to promote the client's gadget contest, a global initiative wherein users were encouraged to develop gadgets/applications for one of the company's products. Their collaboration resulted in 190 gadget submissions.

With the success of HA's blogger campaign, the client decided to extend its community outreach further. In Singapore, HA has now started an engagement program to reach out to a broader audience. It is now working with schools, real estate agents, and travel portals in a bid to introduce relevant applications and to gain a better understanding of the market's level of interaction with the company's various online tools.

Source: The Hoffman Agency.

Meet Joe Blog

The most talked about social media tool since 2004 has to be the blog, short for weblog.

Blogs provide commentary or news on a particular subject; function as personal online diaries; offer a public soapbox to air views; or represent a collaborative space. A typical blog combines text, images, and links to other blogs, websites, and other media related to its topic.

What makes a good blog? Ask a hundred bloggers, get a hundred answers. But some items are common to all responses—a good blog is current and up-to-date; it is open to comments, encourages discussion, and tolerates dissent; it interacts with a community of other bloggers; and helps readers find relevant information. It has something interesting to say, is personal, and, most importantly, has a personality of its own, its unique voice.

Perhaps the most well-known Asian blog in the last few years is that of Rui Chenggang, an anchor on China's CCTV. On January 15, 2007, he posted an entry on his personal blog calling for Starbucks to be evicted from its corner of the Forbidden City in Beijing, where it had had an outlet for six years. The coffee shop, he said, "tramples on Chinese culture" and is "an insult to Chinese civilization."

Within two days, his blog had been bombarded 500,000 times and collected thousands of messages in support. The furor was quickly picked up by China's online and mainstream media, leading to a consumer boycott of the outlet. The authorities in charge of the Forbidden City issued a statement defending their decision to have Starbucks there in the first place and promised a review of its presence within six months. By the end of the week, this had led to a flood of negative coverage in the international media, accusing Starbucks of insensitivity to Chinese nationalist sentiment and to the local environment.

The result? The Starbucks coffee shop closed.

For PR professionals and organizations, this type of reaction makes blogs both appealing and risky. Many companies have used the personal nature of blogs to project a more human, public face and invite direct interaction with customers and even critics. A handful of big-time executives are often cited as examples, such as Cisco Indonesia's Managing Director, Irfan Setiaputra; Tan Kin Lian, retired CEO of NTUC Income in Singapore; and Sanjeev Bikhchandani of Naukri in India. Arguably more important are the hundreds of rank-and-file employees blogging on behalf of their companies, either explicitly or through their personal blogs.

Public relations' role is to work with organization's informal spokespeople and ambassadors to make sure they have relevant topics, a clear set of guidelines, and the support they need to succeed. There are no hard and fast rules about what a blog should be, but most successful bloggers adhere to these guidelines:

Find your niche. An original voice is a big part of standing out, but you also need something interesting to talk about.

Write in your own voice. Be yourself and let your personality show—there is no easier way to demonstrate humanity. If you are scholarly, write like a scholar. If you are a wit, write with humor.

Stifle the instinct to please everyone. Blandness is a blogging death sentence. Part of being a real person in a large community is encountering people who disagree with you. If you have not got an angry comment or two on your blog, you probably have not written anything interesting.

Acknowledge comments, especially dissent. Credibility comes from being able to deal constructively with dissent. If your readers do not sense a real conversation on your blog, they will look for one elsewhere.

Have an opinion. Be candid and tell us how you really feel. One of the best ways to stimulate an engaging discussion is to be a bit provocative.

Be patient. It takes time to build an audience and also for your blogging voice to settle into its natural ground. Be prepared to invest a few months in finding your voice and rhythm.

To blog or not to blog. Public relations professionals face the challenge of demonstrating how blogs effectively support business goals. While blogging's value cannot be measured precisely, like many PR initiatives, they can be considered in terms of their benefits and losses— what benefit will you gain from the blog, most likely in terms of engagement; what is the cost of the blog in terms of hard costs and executive resources; and, of course, what are the risk factors involved and, together with costs, do they outweigh the benefits?

Case Study

Air New Zealand used Chinese celebrities and blogging to increase awareness of its brand and position New Zealand as a destination for the Chinese public.

New Zealand holidays were presented to Chinese celebrities, who in return, updated fans daily with their travel experiences on their Air NZ blog sites. The airline provided them with tailored itineraries to showcase the country's natural beauty, resulting in boosting tourist numbers from China by 20 percent.

Source: Asia Pacific PR Awards 2007.

Engaging with bloggers

How, when, and even if to engage with bloggers has been the topic of much discussion in the PR industry. Some say you should enter the fray and blog away; others take a more cautious approach.

Whatever approach you take, the most important aspect of engagement is to know your bloggers well. You should know if there are influential bloggers in your space and what their point of view is. Some will hold themselves to higher ethical standards than others. You also need to prioritize—there are important bloggers and then there's everyone else.

You can use any search engine to find blogs. Specialized blog search engines can also help you find blogs even when you do not know what they are called—or even knew they existed. You may also find relevant blogs by looking at the "Blogroll" (yes, really), which is a link within a blog to other blogs.

Popular Blog Search Engines

International—www.blogsearchengine.com, and www.technorati.com

Australia—www.theaustralianindex.com

China—www.baidu.com, www.chinabloglist.org

Hong Kong—http://hk.onbloglist.com

India—www.labnol.org/india-blogs

Indonesia—www.bloghub.com/Indonesia

Japan—www.kizasi.co.jp

Korea—www.naver.com, and www.daum.com

Malaysia—www.mycen.com.my/malaysia/blog.html

New Zealand—www.nzs.com/media/blogs

Philippines—http://philippineinternetreview.blogspot.com

Singapore—www.bloggersg.com

Taiwan—http://blog.go2.tw/

Health Warning: Given the speed of change, it is likely that some of the websites or statistics given in this chapter will be out of date by the time the book is published.

Digital Media Tools

Moblogs, vblogs, and podcasting

Blogs have now moved beyond text and graphics. Moblogs are blogs created by contributions from mobile devices such as photographs as well as text, while vblogs add video to the format.

Podcasting is basically a form of audio blogging. Organizations produce radio-style shows or interviews and feed them via RSS. Then you
download them on your iPod or other MP3 player. The continued pop-
ularization of the term "podcast" and the increased availability of content options largely fuel the growth in podcast listening. Organizations
all over Asia Pacific are now using podcasts, including among many,
Malaysia's *CIO* magazine; Radio New Zealand, the *South China Morning
Post, Computerworld Australia*, Cisco Asia, IBM China, the University of
the Philippines, and even Radio Free Asia Lao. Additionally, using podcasts for internal purposes is a great way to test the waters before you
start creating content for customers.

Keep it really simple stupid

Blogs can be read like any other website by going to its URL. However,
nearly all blogs and news sites now offer RSS, which stands for "really simple syndication" and not the above, as is used with humor. It is a form of
programming that allows users to receive select news and updates. In effect,
they have the ability to choose what type of news and information they
want to read and see, and ignore that which is of no interest. These updates
are sent automatically to the user's RSS New Reader, a software program
which acts like an e-mail inbox.

Popular RSS Readers

http://reader.google.com

www.netvibes.com

http://rssbandit.org/

www.newsgator.com/Individuals/FeedDemon

www.newsgator.com/individuals/netnewswire

The good news about RSS is that it filters out unwanted information.
The bad news is that it filters out unwanted information! This filtering

presents a major challenge for the PR profession, which is trying to have its voice heard.

Social bookmarking

Social bookmarking is a growing phenomenon, whereby Internet users can store, organize, search, and manage bookmarks of web pages on the Internet. In a social bookmarking system, users save links to web pages that they want to remember and/or share. These bookmarks are usually public, and bloggers and news sources rely on their content for success. The system is very simple—news stories and websites are submitted by users, and then the sites are promoted to the front page through a user-based ranking system. Popular international social bookmarks are Digg, Reddit, and del.icio.us; while you can also use local tools, such as the Singapore Social Media Directory (sgSocial MediaDir) and Malaysia's Innit.

Something wiki this way comes

In its most basic form, a wiki is a website that supports user collaboration. Once a document or item is created, all the wiki users have the ability to easily create, revise, and update. They also have the ability to engage in some form of discussion about the documents on which they are collaborating.

The best-known example is, of course, Wikipedia, the world's largest online encyclopedia. Wikipedia's rapid ascent is, in large part, a result of being completely user-driven. All of the content is collaboratively developed by writers and editors around the world.

From a public relations point of view, participation in a wiki has to be handled with great care, and sensitivity is needed in order not to enrage the viewers. It has already been shown that organizations as diverse as the US Democrats and Republicans, the Central Intelligence Agency, and the BBC have altered their entries on Wikipedia. During the run-up to the 2007 elections in Australia, the prime minister's office and a host of government departments came under heavy criticism when it was found they had been anonymously contributing and editing entries on Wikipedia. The Australian Defense Department was revealed as the most prolific source of Wikipedia changes, with more than 5,000 traced to its staff.

SEO

The public relations industry is gradually coming to grips with the concept of SEO (search engine optimization) and SERM (search engine reputation management). Professionals are actively utilizing SEO to raise the profile of their organizations or topics on search engine rankings at special times, such as when launching new products or, more importantly, providing detailed information on important issues.

At the heart of most search engines, be it Yahoo!, Baidu, Chol, or Go, is a system called page ranking, which essentially gives every site on the Internet a rank. The page rank of your site is determined by the links to your website. Each time somebody adds a link to your website, the search engine interprets this as a vote for your site. The more links you have to your site, the more votes you get.

The SEO algorithm also analyzes the importance of the website that has cast a vote for you. Obviously, a link from a site with a higher page rank helps your site more. An increase in page rank of only a couple of places can mean the difference between being on page one of the search results and page seven, where nobody may find you. This can be literally the difference between a business venture succeeding or failing.

Of course, page rank is not the only important element of a successful search. Search engines also look for "keywords"—any word someone might type into a search engine to find a website. A "keyword phrase" is a string of words used to describe what the searcher is looking for.

Writers for the Internet are always looking for ways of increasing keywords on their pages—with keywords in the title, in the lead, in the main body of the text, in the description tags, and with the sheer density of keywords in the copy. While Google and Yahoo! are smart enough not to be fooled by just keyword after keyword separated by commas, it does pay strong attention to keyword density.

The way search engines use algorithms to rank sites has major implications for public relations. We have to be careful how we use words—we have to look at their density and positioning. But, then, at what point does writing for the Internet begin to interfere with writing ability and, even more importantly, with journalistic integrity? The challenge for our profession is not only to make SEO work in multiple Asian languages, but also to produce newsworthy, relevant copy that both stimulates and entertains the readers it's aimed at whilst scoring high on searches and, at the same time does not become formulaic text that readers are unlikely to appreciate.

Social media releases

Closely linked to SEO are social media releases. Social media releases are simply media releases which have been formatted so information is easy to scan on a computer; utilizing bullets and lists of ready-made quotes instead of dense text.

When they first entered into the mainstream, there was some feeling that social media releases would mark the end of the traditional media release, which only had static text. However, as with all media outreach, the vehicle has to be appropriate to the receiver. Certainly, journalists working at the more traditional newspapers in Asia and particularly those which still have relatively limited language options on the Internet, will not look kindly on a media release which appears to be aimed at the amateur blogger.

That said, while traditional formats still work particularly well for certain scenarios, social media releases offer new ways for journalists and bloggers to create exciting content. Several PR professionals are advocating a template for social media releases, as outlined below, which still follows the traditional pyramid structure of a media release.

1. Contact information
2. Headline
3. Core facts—in bullet points
4. Multimedia materials such as photos, video, graphics, or audio files
5. Spokesperson quotations
6. Links to recent coverage
7. Boilerplate
8. RSS feed to the organizations' website and media release pages
9. Links and tags for social bookmarks and RSS

Social Media Minefields

Today's flow of information takes local issues global and helps global issues find local relevance, often within hours of that first blog posting or text message chain. Communities that span continents, age groups, and backgrounds can be created at the speed of light, with a few clicks of the mouse, and are often galvanized around specific issues. Citizen journalists, bloggers, and net groups regularly break a story—think Dell China's "Processorgate."

This power can take an issue to its boiling point before a company even knows a problem exists. China has had its fair share of food and consumer goods crises and the problems facing Colgate China in 2005, when its Total toothpaste was incorrectly reported to contain a cancer-causing agent, demonstrates the power of the medium. It all started from one small article in the *Standard* newspaper in the UK, which reported on research conducted at the Virginia Institute of Technology in the United States. The report said that the studies had proven that the antibacterial agent, triclosan, which is contained in Colgate Total, produces a harmful, cancer-causing, and potentially fatal, chloroform gas when combined with chlorinated water. That same weekend, China's *Legal Evening News*, one of the country's most influential newspapers, picked up on the coverage. The newspaper headlined with: "British media say Colgate toothpastes contain a cancer-causing chemical."

That resulted in a deluge of coverage in the newspapers, on TV, online, and via mobile texting. Before Colgate knew it, everyone seemed to be texting, e-mailing, and blogging about the news. One week after the initial report, surveys showed that consumer confidence in Colgate had dropped to nearly zero and in-store sales of all Colgate products were plummeting by up to 50 percent. Colgate, of course, mobilized an international and effective public relations strategy to deal with the crisis, finding out the truth of the erroneous report, meeting with government officials to reassure them, and implementing media outreach at all levels, particularly with influential China Internet portals such as www.sina.com. The company met with great success; restoring its reputation and market share.

Case Study

In early 2008, Upstream Asia was given a challenging assignment; amid the fast growing but fiercely competitive China automobile market, help Fiat re-launch Italy's legendary automotive brand with a communications program leading up to the Beijing Auto Show 2008. The objective was to take the initiative, influence the agenda, and move coverage of Fiat beyond corporate news to focus on the modern, European values of the brand; in particular, Fiat's global environmental leadership.

In the first half of 2008, as the world's fastest growing major automotive market, every significant market player focused on the Beijing show to create an impact. And many chose to appeal to a growing sense of environmental awareness among China's car-owning middle class. In the lead-up to the show, Fiat's challenge was to cut through the clutter and stand out from the crowd.

While other brands chose to focus on their own competing environmental technologies, for Fiat this was only the beginning. Fiat's eco:Drive application, being shown in China for the first time, enables drivers to gauge the environmental friendliness of their style of driving.

This inspired a clear, differentiated point of view for Fiat: that *it's not only the car that you drive, but the way that you drive that has a real impact on the environment.*

Digital tools then enabled Upstream to make this original and insightful viewpoint relevant to the local market.

In the space of just one week, the Fiat communications team worked with leading Chinese portal www.sina.com to develop a research project to understand Chinese car owners' perceptions about the link between driving style and fuel efficiency. Where in the past, consumer research would have taken months, the online survey was designed, implemented, and results compiled within ten days.

Questions were designed to link directly back to Fiat and the eco:Drive system. The online methodology enabled targeted, efficient research and fast turnaround, while the report's conclusions supported Fiat's eco: Drive technology.

Fiat's unique point of view regarding the environment was key to determining the scope and content of the survey. Digital tools enabled the team to deploy quickly and effectively. The results of research then formed the basis of a concentrated media outreach, including a pre-show workshop for the media, which set the scene for the launch of Fiat's cars at the show. *(Continued)*

The outreach campaign around the eco:Drive initiative during the Beijing Auto Show 2008 alone generated more than 100 monitored media impressions. Of these:

- 57 percent were online media coverage
- 43 percent were traditional print media coverage
- 15 percent recognized Fiat's expertise in the environmentally responsible driving field, and its global leadership in this arena

Source: Upstream Asia.

Social Networks

It is said that you simply cannot understand the emotional appeal or the rational value delivered by social networking sites until you participate. Ask anyone on Facebook, Twitter or MySpace sites, or any of the local Asian sites such as Mixi in Japan, Heyspace in Hong Kong, or merepasand in India, and they will endorse this opinion.

Looking specifically at Facebook, the tool was originally a series of private networks for colleges and high schools. But then the company decided that anyone could join—and that anyone could create mini-applications or widgets for the site. That led to an explosion of new members and new applications, letting more people create more custom sites for themselves. The networks and groups, in particular, are as varied as they are numerous, ranging from country sites such as Singapore, Malaysia, India, and Hong Kong, with hundreds of thousands of members, to more specialist groups ranging from the practical—such as the "PR Networkers"—to the whimsical, including "In praise of the wasabi pea." Facebook overtook Chinese language social networks such as Xanga and UWants as the top social network with a 37.72 percent share in Hong Kong in January 2008.

Clearly, these networks represent an extraordinary opportunity for public relations. However, as organizations embrace and begin to interact with the social-networking public, there is the increased risk that they will attract critics concerned about controversial material posted either in those groups or by members of a company's group that has posted offensive material elsewhere.

In 2007, two social networking groups, one on Facebook belittling Islam and the other on MySpace criticizing the military, caused significant protest. More than 66,000 members joined a petition threatening to quit Facebook if the anti-Islam group was not deleted. The anti-troops group on MySpace garnered a similar petition. However, many groups, almost identical to those deleted, remain on Facebook, proving how pervasive caustic commentary is on social networking sites.

Almost 60 percent of Facebook's users are now outside the United States. And by the end of 2008, Asia was projected to have the largest share of social networking users, at 35 percent, according to research firm Datamonitor. Most of the social networks are, therefore, looking to expand their offerings. Google's first India-based networking site, Orkut, which debuted in 2004, has gained traction in the sub-continent and is becoming increasingly popular in other Asian countries. Facebook also plans to make its web pages available in languages other than English in 2008, as the networking site targets new users in Asia and beyond.

How exactly organizations can utilize social networks is still open for debate. Supporting company groups and special interest forums is a way into the mix. However, like blogging, organizations need to remain transparent at all times and not appear to encroach on the freedom and flexibility of the networkers.

Virtual Lifestyles

Finally, how to work with virtual realities such as Second Life and China's HiPiHi is a thorny topic of conversation for the PR professional. While already looking like yesterday's technology, there are many successful examples of effective public relations activity on Second Life. Sun Microsystems holds the record as the first Fortune 500 company to hold a virtual media conference on Second Life, to show off its "newly-built" product and brand pavilion.

Although Second Life is beginning to launch Asian sites, such as in Japan and Korea, for many organizations the sheer effort of building a presence on Second Life has been insurmountable. This is one reason why HiPiHi scores well in China. HiPiHi audiences are young (20-30 years old) and new to the 3D worlds, while Second Life attracts a more mature, tech-savvy audience in its 30s. Many firms will be waiting for similar sites to open in their own markets before taking the plunge.

Case Study

Chinese brand TCL, one of the largest manufacturers in the global television industry, sought to help Chinese consumers better understand HDTV while raising its own profile and that of Chinese TV brands overall. It had three clear campaign objectives:

- Re-position itself as a reliable, fashionable, high-end manufacturer of HD LCD TVs
- Improve perceptions of Chinese brands
- Boost sales of HD LCD TVs

In 2007, Burson-Marsteller and TCL conceived a social media-based review campaign that would involve ordinary families, utilizing the theme that "upgrading to a HD/LCD TV allows families to spend happier times together at home." Consumers drove the marketing campaign with free reign to publicly post genuine, uncensored comments and feedback about the product and the brand through blogs and an online forum.

A "100 Happy Families Blog Competition" selected 100 families from 11 cities across China from among 660 applications. Families received a free TCL HD LCD TV for one month and using a dedicated website and forum to blog about their experiences, created a potent viral marketing and word-of-mouth campaign as families directed everyone in their social networks to the website to vote. Finalist families won a trip to Lijiang, China, where one lucky family won a big screen TCL HD LCD TV.

Throughout the campaign, celebrities and senior media editors provided endorsements and attracted media interest. Consumer touchpoints, including interactive blogs and call centers, were established to promote two-way communication between TCL and consumers and to leverage their strong individual networks.

Success was measured according to four factors:

- Consumer Engagement: Nearly 700 applicant families, half a million page views, and over a quarter million consumer votes
- Media Responsiveness: More than 200 pieces of coverage generated with AVE (Advertising Value Equivalency) of nearly US$ 200,000
- Pre and post Campaign Research: Three times as many online voters said they would select a Chinese LCD TV and more than

(Continued)

90 percent had greater confidence in the TCL brand than before the campaign

- Impact on Sales: As of August 2007 sales grew 69 percent compared to the same period in 2006

Source: Burson-Marsteller and TCL.

Resistance is Useless

It would be hard to think of another time in the history of public relations when there were more challenges or opportunities. In just a short amount of time, digital and social media have made a big splash. Perhaps the most significant indicator of social media's importance is recognizing it has become embedded into the traditional media. *Korea Herald* and *Straits Times* journalists now have their own blogs.

We have already said goodbye to the posthumously named Web 1.0 era, when communication was largely one-way from the content creators, and we are now in the middle of the Web 2.0 phase, with millions of consumers calling the shots. Full-blown interactivity is the way things are as Asian stakeholders across a range of demographic bands are sourcing and creating their own realities.

What can we expect from Web 3.0?

We can certainly expect faster downloads, higher resolution images and video, and new minority groups to find their voice. But we can also anticipate new and more exciting ways for individuals and groups to communicate with each other, in ways we cannot even imagine yet.

However, even though we recognize the changes brought about by this new, digital world, this evolution is still less to do with digital tools and interactive channels, and more to do with the way in which it allows organizations to engage with their stakeholders. It is about earning credibility and, crucially, trust—and not just having the same monologue through new multiple channels. This is no different than before—it is just that channels are faster and more interactive.

Digital and social media are not yet seen as a replacement for traditional media and, most importantly, personal contact. Social media will continue to operate in conjunction with traditional media and traditional public relations practices. So, convergence of communication medium, method, and practice seem to be the order of the day.

So, what can the public relations profession do to ensure we continue to leverage and utilize the digital medium?

1. We need to understand the rules of what works and what does not.

2. We need to be communicating consistently—not just when there is an issue.

3. We should not replace traditional media with digital as they still serve as a vital information channel, entertainment base, and communication source. Rather, we need to expand our horizons to achieve the best mix.

4. We need to be at the forefront of new technologies and enablers, but not so far ahead that we leave our audience behind.

5. We need to continually monitor what is being said about our organization so we can be proactive or reactive appropriately.

6. And, lastly, we need to find out what the audience cares about, so we can provide them with what they want.

CHAPTER 13

You'll Never Walk Alone

Integrated and All-Embracing PR

Public relations professionals never walk or work alone—they are always cast in the role of the linking agents between the organization and the stakeholders. They are now even more interconnected on a professional level with the other members of the marketing communications mix as the trend is firmly that of taking an integrated marcoms approach to implement most promotional activities. The public relations effort can be seen as the "cement" that holds communications programs together.

In times of economic downturn, this is even more pertinent—and, in fact, this approach was born of the 1989 global recession when advertising agencies and public relations consultancies were engaged in mergers with large media organizations—a trend that has continued to this day and will continue with rapidity as the world faces the biggest economic meltdown in 2009 since post World War 2.

As PR professionals are trained in seeing opportunity in every challenge, then this is not a time to drop off the planet or run for the hills. The truth is that in times of economic uncertainty, we need to engage in public relations activities more than ever as companies across Asia will need to protect their brand equity and corporate reputation in an increasingly hostile and challenging marketplace simply in order to survive.

Toward Integration

In the past two decades small-, medium-, and large-scale enterprises globally and across Asia Pacific have been turning to a more holistic, integrated approach in meeting their communication challenges. Integrated marketing communication or integrated communications refers to the selective use of combined communications—promotions, public relations, sales, and advertising—to position the brand and develop sustainable relationships with stakeholders over time based on a collective voice.

"A healthy offspring of two parents: marketing and PR, MPR [marketing public relations] represents an opportunity for companies to regain a share of voice in a message satiated society. MPR not only delivers a strong share of voice to win a strong share of mind and heart; it also delivers a better, more effective voice in many cases," so says Philip Kotler.[1]

This integrated marketing communication approach creates avenues of awareness so that public relations in combination with advertising, for example, will make your presence felt and take your message to the target stakeholders or a range of them. This integrated approach will ensure that information about the product, company, issue, or brand is disseminated in a holistic way so that awareness is raised, engagement is established, and a favorable impression is left with key stakeholders.

Case Study

Wrigley is a leader in the confectionery industry and the world's largest manufacturer and marketer of chewing gum.

In 2005, Wrigley China wanted to boost sales and strengthen the brand image and share of voice for its "Extra White" chewing gum. Burson-Marsteller's nationwide *"Extra White Brilliant Smile"* campaign aimed to transform Wrigley Extra White into a preferred lifestyle choice, through a nationwide integrated PR, advertising, retail, and sampling campaign.

Wrigley's campaign objectives were to boost product sales by building a brand proposition more relevant to consumers through:

1. Strengthening the premium, modern, and elegant brand image of Extra White
2. Deepening Extra White's brand value
3. Raising the brand's share of voice

(Continued)

The strategy determined was:

- Focus on Extra White consumers' desire to feel attractive by emphasizing an emotional end-benefit: white teeth make a pleasant smile
- Use "Smile" as a colorful lifestyle cue to communicate the key messages
- Leverage a brand-building program and roll out marketing activities to stimulate market growth

Wrigley's Extra White Brilliant Smile Competition allowed consumers to showcase their smiling faces on large, public LED screens across China, competing to win "dream-come-true" colorful life experiences. The campaign was supported by online and offline advertising, a special website, and an intense media relations outreach. Through online voting in public arenas and at home, five competition entrants won colorful prizes from five different color groups: Red—Romance; Orange—Passion; Blue—Dreams; Green—Hope; and White—grand prize and color of a Brilliant, Extra-White Smile.

The *Brilliant Smile* campaign results were outstanding:

- Over 3 million visitors to photo stations
- 47,028 photos captured
- 46,000 smile photo entries and over 470,000 votes on the *Brilliant Smile* website
- 192 articles, 618 million media impressions, and US$770,000 in AVE
- 60,000+ customer database for future marketing efforts
- Brand awareness July–September 2005 up 28 percent
- Purchase intention and behavior up 35 percent
- All five attributes of brand equity increased significantly in the third quarter of 2005 versus other quarters
- Campaign communicated the brand proposition and enhanced dental equity

Extra White SOM (sale of merchandise) steadily increased in modern trade channels across China by 4 percent and above, and in key cities by 8.7 percent.

Source: Wrigley China and Burson-Marsteller, Guangzhou.

PR Comes into Its Own

A number of recent factors have enabled public relations to sit at the marketing table as an equal, or maybe more than an equal. These include rising advertising costs and declining mass audiences, global economic downturns, growing costs of sales forces, increasingly segmented media, and the need to build and sustain brand and corporate awareness in the minds and hearts of customers for ultimate survival.

Public relations offers effective, versatile solutions to establish stakeholder awareness and engagement in a variety of attention-getting and interesting ways ensuring wide exposure of the issue, the product, the service, or the organization.

Public relations is eminently suited to leading the IMC (integrated marketing communications) approach due to the following reasons:

1. PR focuses on developing long-lasting relationships through genuine stakeholder support and fully understands the need to develop and implement two-way or multi-leveled communications between an organization or a brand and its stakeholders.

2. Organizations cannot survive without developing and maintaining good relationships with their stakeholders. This transcends the simple sales-driven relationship. It means dealing with issues of concern to stakeholders and managing the broader environmental influences in sectors such as healthcare, financial relations, and technology.

3. In life, things cannot really be achieved alone. A strategic plan must be multi-leveled to respond to the complexities of communications problems. Collaboration must be activated at both the strategic and tactical levels in integrated communications driven by the PR plan. Advertising may control the message; marketing and product promotion supports this. Public relations adds value to this dynamic by building and sustaining credibility for, and trust in, the brand and the organization behind it. In this way, PR builds the brand, creates the buzz, and sustains the customer relationship through credible communication.

4. PR is all about developing and sustaining relationships through understanding the consumer cognitively, and affectively and precisely how and why they respond to key messages. The promotional communicator's message is behavorial change—if the consumer does not respond, then the communications effort fails. PR can lead the integrated communications approach and be all embracing in its strategy and tactics because it listens to the voice of the market and responds with an integrated arsenal of communication tools directly or via third-party endorsers to get the message across, create the buzz, and make it happen.

5. Integrated communications is all about understanding consumers and their needs so that organizations can anticipate and respond to them in a timely fashion. That is the essence of the PR effort.

There is no room for solo performances in the competitive marketplace. The message must be communicated harmoniously by a choir of integrated voices.

Revisiting PR as a One-Stop Shop

Now, public relations agencies and professionals can offer one-stop communications solutions and use helicopter vision to view their organization's communication needs. In response to the findings of this needs based research, they can choose from a potpourri of PR tools—taking a veritable Asian buffet-style approach. In adopting a strategic approach to the PR program, both below the line and above the line approaches can be integrated to provide impactful communications solutions resulting in gaining favorable stakeholder recognition for an organization's efforts. Essentially, the corporate or brand message needs to be communicated consistently to the customer as a means of keeping the relationship alive. In strategically and selectively deploying key aspects of the communications mix according to the situation, public relations remains adaptive and all-inclusive—being all things to all organizations.

Case Study

"What's Your Personalitea?" campaign by Ogilvy PR for PT Unilever Indonesia set out to raise awareness of its newly launched Sariwangi Powder Range, the first powdered tea range in the Indonesian market. A unique market position had to be devised for Sariwangi to eradicate big competition and to grab customers' attention.

A strategy was created that was founded on a notion of "the four temperaments," where human personalities can be characterized as sanguine, choleric, melancholic, or phlegmatic. The aim of the PR campaign was to build a social and emotional link between customers and their peers, connecting them to the typical range of personalities they might meet day-by-day, while helping them to develop emotional connections with the people in their daily lives.

The new "What's Your Personalitea?" product line included, Sariwangi's "Sociable Ginger," "Calming Milk," "Motivating Honey," and "Energetic Lime" modeled on real people that the consumer might meet everyday.

The integrated marketing campaign breathed life into the Personalitea concept, including a Personalitea booklet that included a quiz to enable readers identify their Personalitea, while at the same time connecting the benefits of each product to their individual personality.

Mini-quizzes placed in advertorials encourage readers to discover their own personality in terms of the product. An interactive radio chat show enabled listeners to express their personality or their moods on air.

The health benefits of each tea lay at the heart of each narrative and they revealed how an individual's tea selection may provide insights about their deeper personalities. Ongoing coverage of the concept in the media was sustained with a media launch-cum-talk-show followed by a media writing competition. Also for wider and targeted reach, SMS (short message service) blasts promised a free sample to try out.

Source: Asia Pacific PR Awards 2006.

Endnote

1. Kotler, P., *Marketing for Nonprofit Organizations* (Englewood Cliffs, NJ: Prentice Hall, 1982).

14

Measuring Achievement

210 delegate attendees

41 newspaper and magazine articles

5 items of TV and radio broadcast news

Featured in 124 blogs, newsrooms, and social relationship websites

But was the campaign a success?

Tools for measuring public relations campaigns have been around for de-cades. It would be hard to find a public relations professional in Asia Pacific who does *not* utilize some system or another for evaluating their work. These systems range from basic media measurement to sophisticated mod-els that evaluate the long-term psychological and physical response of the audience. It is apparent why measurement and evaluation are so important. If we refer back to chapter 1, how can we hope to gain "Acknowledge-ment of Achievement" if we cannot prove our achievement? Proving cau-sality is a necessity. These days, companies are looking for measurable returns on their investment. With growing pressures on budgets, it has become more important than ever to move beyond the anecdotal and informal evaluation and to demonstrate a tangible benefit, be it through increased sales, higher share price, or more recruits.

Then, of course, measurement and evaluation is part of the never-ending planning cycle: planning—implementation—evaluation—planning... and so on.

However, even if we see a clear result, how can we know whether it was due to the public relations effort or to other environmental factors, including advertising, direct marketing, and even word of mouth? For example, was an IPO successful because of the investor relations effort, or was it due to corporate finance's road show? It may never be possible to report this precisely.

But the public relations profession should take heart—the same agonizing takes place in the offices of advertisers and other marketing disciplines. And, of course, the answer is that all factors play a part; it's rare to be in a position to evaluate a project purely on the basis of one element. This is why setting sensible and measurable objectives at the very start is so important.

The "IOIO" Model of Measurement

In looking at measurement, the majority of systems are based on what we refer to as the "IOIO" model of measuring input, output, impact, and outcome:

Input—a measure of the quantity of activity undertaken

Output—a measure of the immediate results of what has been produced

Impact—measuring the effect of the output on the target audience

Outcome—how the program has impacted the business objective

For example:

Input	Output	Impact	Outcome
Media releases	Media coverage	Positive awareness	Sales
Speaking engagements	Audience response	Product enquiries	Market share
Legislator meetings	Meeting feedback	Support of company issue	Legislative changes

While most evaluation programs are conducted on a long-term business basis, the diagram above demonstrates that it is equally important to know what you want to achieve through any specific activity. Every activity—whether it is a media interview, a stakeholder meeting, a new product launch, or an issues management project—has an underlying business objective. For example, if one of your sub-strategies is to reach consumers who read the weekend edition of the *Wall Street Journal Asia*, then it is perfectly acceptable to set the number and quality of articles appearing in that medium as a goal for evaluation.

Over the years, several writers, from Grunig and Cutlip, to Center and Broom, have theorized different versions of the basic model. For our region, perhaps the best-known measurement master is Jim Macnamara, who heads the Asia Pacific franchise of CARMA. He introduced his "Pyramid Model of PR Research," which essentially looks at the IOIO model as a bottom-up pyramid structure, demonstrating the evaluation process from the initial strategy and activities, to the final outcomes.[1]

Point of View

"The use of research in public relations programs is growing at around 14 percent a year, according to the Association for Measurement and Evaluation of Communication; compared with 7–8 percent growth in PR generally. This signals a growing acceptance of measurement and evaluation. But the industry started from a low base. While it is claimed that barriers are cost and time, the real steps to go forward are increasing education of practitioners in communication theory and research, and further integration of PR into management reporting."

Dr. Jim Macnamara, Professor of Public Communication,
University of Technology, Sydney

While outcome will always, by necessity, be on a case-by-case assessment basis, we have several tools for evaluating general output and impact, as outlined below.

Advertising Value Equivalency (AVE)

Mention advertising value equivalency to a public relations professional— that is, calculating the advertising value equivalent of the space or time of editorial coverage—and you will most likely be greeted with a sneer and a comment about how this form of measurement does not really get to the heart of quality.

True. Editorial and advertising are not directly comparable. One of the founding tenets of our industry is the view that editorial is more credible than advertising because it is produced by a third party, the media, who are, in theory, independent and objective. In addition, while advertising can be assumed to be positive for a company, media coverage may be negative or, at best, neutral. Editorial often contains references to more than one company and, of course, sometimes contains errors or factual inaccuracies, which is, hopefully, not present in advertising.

It is possible to weight AVE based on factors relating to the quality of the editorial. However, there is little scientific evidence to back this up at present, and is in danger of being taken too seriously.

However, despite the negative perception of AVE, it can certainly have a place in evaluation, particularly when budget for measurement is tight. It can present a helpful guide to the ROI (return on investment) and determine where funds should be directed in future. Where it works best is when it is considered as part of a "balanced scorecard" approach; used as just one element of measurement along with other tools.

Media Analysis

The most prolific tool of measurement in public relations is tracking coverage in the media. We are, however, far beyond simply counting clippings or broadcast coverage. We are also looking for the quality of the editorial, for example:

- Dominance and share of voice—whether the item covers just the organization or refers to several organizations
- Size or length of item
- Photographs, graphics, and logos
- Position or time in media outlet, such as the front or back of a newspaper; the first or last item in a news broadcast
- Favorability and tone of the article
- Importance of the media outlet to the target audience
- Coverage of the key messages of the campaign

These days, there are several global firms offering sophisticated media analysis packages, based on ever-evolving software. These are, in fact, all based on the basic numerical system of allocating points to the above criteria, which was used quite often in our region in the early 1990s. The new systems go far beyond a points-allocation, however, by ranking all the factors according to pre-assigned variables.

When we talk about media measurement we are, of course, including digital media—news sites, websites, chat rooms, networking sites, and the rest. The same criteria used in analyzing print and broadcast articles can be applied equally to postings on the Internet, looking at page views, time spent on pages, and click-throughs. The advantage of tracking digital media is, of course, that much of it can be done from the desktop, using various news search systems, including Bloomberg, Factiva, and conducting a simple Google search. Most media monitoring firms in Asia Pacific, such as Cision, offer digital measurement along with the more traditional print and broadcast measurement, while some firms such as Meltwater News specialize only in online media.

The proliferation of digital media has, naturally, made it difficult to track coverage and evaluate one media outlet against another. In most cases we find ourselves undertaking double bottom-line reporting, with stories from traditional media being repeated or re-shaped for the Internet. In fact, it is not uncommon for one major company we know in Asia Pacific to receive in excess of 3,000 traditional and online media hits each month—in multiple languages. It is not practical to track every item of coverage nor allocate the resources to conducting this scale of detailed analysis; not to mention finding someone who is willing to read a report of that size.

In addition, we need to recognize that our media habits are changing. We do not consume media in isolation—we are likely to learn about the same story in several different formats, including newspapers, on TV, and online. This makes it all the harder to measure the impact.

Despite this sounding like a Herculean task, media analysis will almost certainly remain the dominant form of measurement for the foreseeable future. Indeed, if a publication is considered of particular importance to a program strategy, then there is no reason why evaluating its coverage of a topic should not be a prime measurement factor. However, as with AVE, media measurement is best used when used as part of a complete measurement kit.

Research

Research, be it quantitative or qualitative, is a popular tool for public relations, based on comparing variables before and after a campaign. Current perceptions and behavior of our audience can be measured by conducting research to establish a benchmark prior to a PR program, followed up by a post-test to determine how effective the program has been.

In the past, surveys could be quite time consuming and costly, even if taking part on the back of an "omnibus" survey; that is a survey carried out by a research firm on behalf of several companies who are allocated a certain number of questions each. There was resistance to this type of research; after all, no one wants to spend most of the budget on measurement.

These days, however, we tend to use online methods—there are many companies, which offer inexpensive online packages, which can be administered directly with results coming directly to the company. These packages are available on a global basis, but common companies used in this region include SurveyMonkey, ConstantContact, and PollDaddy.

Similar to advertising, public relations can also make use of focus groups, either formal or informal, to test out new organizational directions and generate more in-depth insights into stakeholder perceptions. Strategies and creative ideas can be pre-tested in small focus groups—be they especially invited members or informal employee or media groups.

Finally, away from the time-consuming survey research, it is common for public relations professionals to conduct a straw poll among the media to determine knowledge and sentiment, which will help direct the PR program strategy.

An Integrated Approach

In considering how to measure a public relations program, there are two key tenets we should keep in mind:

As we saw in chapter 2, we need to establish clear, strategic program objectives that are measurable, using numbers and dates that are not vague or addressing unquantifiable hopes. Without these concrete and specific objectives, there can be no measurement and no evaluation. The objectives should ideally be framed in both long-term, that is outcomes, and short-term, that is outputs.

Second, we should consider using more than one measurement tool at a time. There is not just one tool that will accurately calculate the value of public relations, but a combination of metrics such as media analysis, AVE, and some top-line research can give us a good picture of what we have achieved through our programs.

Given the importance of measurement and evaluation, it is surprising how few major public relations consultancies discuss this on their websites or promotional materials. We found that only five of the top 20 or so global firms talked in any detail about measurement. Try it for yourself.

In an ideal world, it would be beneficial for the industry to adopt standard evaluation criteria for measuring campaigns. In this way, we can benchmark the success of programs across industries and media and meet the growing demand for a clearer ROI. Of course, due to the varied nature of public relations, it is unrealistic to think we can create an evaluation tool that provides a "one-size-fits-all" solution. That said, certain elements of measurement could be standardized—media analysis and AVE being likely candidates. Several organizations, including the US-based Institute for Public Relations and the UK's Public Relations Consultants Association have published guidelines for measuring public relations, which, although a long way from becoming industry-standard, are at least a step in the right direction.

If the trend for tighter budgets continues, so will the need for evaluation from companies who want to see their investment fully justified and more accountable. For them, it is not just a case of "what gets measured gets done." Instead, it is "what gets measured proves that it has been done"— and hopefully is done well. At the end of the day, if the public relations profession is to continue to grow credibility, proving causality is a must.

Endnote

1. Macnamara, J., *Public Relations Handbook, 5th ed.* (Broadway: Archipelago Press, 2005).

CHAPTER 15

Future Trends for Public Relations in Asia Pacific

Public relations professionals are well versed in crystal ball gazing—after all, being the eyes and ears of the organizations that they counsel, this is what they are expected to do. In planning public relations programs, as we saw in chapter 2, we are trained to examine what has gone before in an organization's history and map out where the organization is right now, to get a handle on where it will be going in the future.

Attempting to analyze public relations across the Asia Pacific region based on its past, present, and future state is beset with complexity, when you factor in the cultural, linguistic, political, and economic differences across some of the largest and smallest populations, active and inactive markets, richest and poorest nations, most educated and undereducated countries on earth. Added to which, the industry itself comprises many parts that make up the whole; each with its own challenges from consultancy and in-house issues, to the specialist sectors of financial, IT, healthcare, and environmental public relations.

This book has addressed both the diverse and the common themes beyond language, ethnicity, ideology, location, and industry that bind together public relations practice in Asia Pacific. This chapter will continue this approach on a futuristic theme to address the issues now facing the profession.

Directions for Asia Pacific PR: Past, Present, and Future

Asia Pacific public relations, in both the public and private sector, is changing due to socioeconomic development and the fast-paced expansion of digital information infrastructures. The shift from nation-building to market development in many emerging democracies and evolving markets across the region including Vietnam, the Philippines and Indonesia is resulting in a move from the government information campaign-style program to more private sector public relations consultancy work.

Elsewhere in Asia Pacific, with the move to more marketization, emerging middle classes, manufacturing bases, and trade expansion, we see countries such as China and India with burgeoning multinational investments requiring more public relations, marketing communications and advertising work for media relations and generic promotional initiatives.

Other countries across the region such as Hong Kong, Australia, and Japan have, in the past few decades, acquired regional interdependence on the back of developed stock markets, the privatization of government-supported organizations, and the globalization of local businesses seeking capital investments in international markets. Public relations in these locations is highly advanced and sophisticated. Here public relations activities are geared to operating successfully in both good and bad economic periods; when investor relations, community relations alongside issues and crisis management are a staple requirement of organizational communications management. In these localities, public relations is utilized to define the organization's position in the market based on strategic relationship building with sophisticated audiences. This is the market model benchmark that all Asia Pacific countries are aiming for—beyond their developing economies and developing democracies—when the widespread use of strategic public relations and stakeholder engagement will mark their economic, social, and political coming-of-age.

Where PR is now

Back in 1993, the Public Relations Society of America, in a report on the future role of public relations, noted,

> Public relations will either become recognized as an indispensable key to all organizations' viability or it will be relegated to merely carrying out a range

of useful techniques. There is evidence that since 1980, while the field has grown greatly in number of practitioners, the majority of additions have been at the tactical level.[1]

Point of View

"Effective communication skills will never be out of fashion. It's a skill set that will always be desired whether you're being interviewed by the media, communicating on Facebook or appear as a hologram. People often say how our next generation prefers to communicate hiding behind their computers. I believe this is why it'll be even more important people maintain their skills so that they are just as comfortable communicating in person as they are online."

Linda Lee, Communications Coach/Trainer, Acewood Group

Nothing lasts forever or stays the same. Today, the role of the public relations professional is no longer marginalized. Although the industry throughout the region has been facing another round of mergers and acquisitions, downsizings and consolidation, public relations professionals will never be more in need by their clients and more busy guiding them through the everyday challenges of surviving in the business environment. Information still needs to be disseminated about these changes, and stakeholder relationships maintained and managed like never before. In fact, the counseling role of the professional will be most requested at this time as part of the corporate survival strategy. This recalls Bernays' visionary projections for the industry back in the early 20th century, which is now the order of the day:

> At first we called our activity "publicity direction." We intended to give advice to our clients on how to direct their actions to get public visibility for them. But, within a year we changed the service and its name to, "counsel on public relations." We recognized that all actions of a client that impinged on the public needed counsel.[2]

Where PR is going

Looking into the crystal ball, we can identify the following three areas that will drive the future for the public relations industry throughout Asia Pacific:

- PR Professional's Performance
- PR Stakeholder Perceptions
- PR Toolbox: Digital Platforms

The performance of PR professionals

Having toyed with name changes from perception managers to corporate communication experts, the term public relations is back in fashion. It underlines the fact that the profession involves more than writing media releases and counting media clippings to justify its impact. Public relations is about engaging with stakeholders to understand their needs and update them about areas of mutual concern using targeted communication messages and tools. In this transactional communications process, the organization should receive acknowledgment of their achievements—to be celebrated by both organization and stakeholder together—both reading from the same page and singing the same song.

The age of communication overload in which we are now situated requires professionals to assist in interpreting and repackaging information enabling organizations to do business and maintain a competitive position or survive in the marketplace whatever the economic climate or geographic location. If you appreciate that the average person today encounters more information in their daily newspaper than their 17th century equivalent did in a lifetime, then the need to be able to select, manage, and create compelling data to get your message out to the appropriate stakeholder is more than apparent.

The value of effective, internally- and externally-focused communication as part of the strategic management plan is now well recognized in the global and regional boardroom and has raised recognition for the profession to greater heights of corporate need. Bernays' public relations counselor, in-house or agency-based, providing daily strategic communications guidance to CEOs across Asia Pacific is now an established reality.

The profession certainly has to walk the talk on CSR. Ethical public relations practices are also under scrutiny globally in specific sectors such as financial and political public relations. The question is who will be responsible for implanting these codes of practice—self-regulation by the industry itself and related professional bodies or external stakeholders? This may be an issue upon which professionals will be intent, in order to influence their own future direction.

A related issue, in terms of the need to self-assess the profession, is that of professional education. While professional associations such as the Council of Public Relations Firms of Hong Kong (CPRF) and the International Association of Business Communicators (IABC) in Singapore and Australia are active, running professional development workshops and seminars, the wider regional spread would validate and professionalize public relations in more developing nations such as Vietnam, Malaysia, India, China, and Indonesia.

PR stakeholders Pressure for change also emerges from increasingly specialized professionals and more educated stakeholder groups who are more demanding in their need for engagement based on timely, relevant, and accurate information about organizations, activities from healthcare and investor relations to consumer and environmental affairs. In addition, the transformative impact of digital communications media cannot be overlooked in terms of changing the profession's ways of connecting with key audiences and managing the media.

PR toolbox—digital platforms How we communicate in terms of sending and receiving information has radically changed in recent times because of the digital communication infrastructures such as the Internet that provide instantaneous global connectivity.

The linear, centralized communication message flow that characterized public relations efforts in the 20th century from one organization to many audiences has shifted to a more distributed, two-way communications model that sees more control in the hands of the receiver. From Internet and SMS usage to the social networking trends of instant messaging, blogs, and wikis, the stakeholder is communication empowered and is actively managing their own communication universe. Public relations professionals will have to fully tap into this digital universe by understanding the best tools to communicate with specific groups based on an understanding of why and how they are used. Essentially, this means more channels can be used to engage stakeholders from consumers to pressure groups, and it requires an even more developed knowledge of their attitudes and behaviors—based on insightful research.

PR in the Age of Social Media Report Commissioned by Council of Public Relations Firms Analyzes the Impact of Social Media on the Industry, July 2007

The US Council of Public Relations Firms (Council), www.prfirms.org, based in New York issued a white paper recently exploring the changing impact that social media communication tools and platforms are having on the public relations industry.

The paper, "Relating to the Public: The Evolving Role of Public Relations in the Age of Social Media," examines the significance of social media including blogs, social networks, and wikis for public relations industry issues, from professional development to client-consultancy relationships and the highly contested competitive marketing services sector.

Some of the main findings of the survey are:

- The public relations industry is well situated to succeed in the realm of social media as public relations has always been in the business of influencing stakeholders

- There is a feeling that the industry should respond quickly and grab its opportunities to maintain its hold alongside other marketing disciplines and to protect its growth

The paper also gathered intelligence from a survey of Council member firms, which substantiated the observable trends taking place within public relations companies in the US.

Some key points arising from that survey covered:

- 84 percent of firms are actively involved in blogosphere for their clients

- 78 percent of participating member firms stated that clients were interested (38 percent) to extremely interested (40 percent) in their social media potential

- Almost half (49 percent) have their own online/interactive group. While an additional 17 percent planned to access this capability inside a year

Source: www.prfirms.org

The advent and widespread use of digital communication technologies provides creative channels to connect with stakeholders. It offers alternatives to the well-worn media pitches, launch events, and product giveaways. Yet, the traditional communication skills—writing, listening, and speaking—are still required to devise and implement effective public relations efforts and nurture stakeholder relationships. It starts and ends with keeping those connections and relationships sweet—whatever the communication vehicles. They are tools of the PR trade and a means to a very important end—enabling professionals to keep ahead of developments and do better, more planned, and interactive public relations.

Point of View

"As Asia's reputation in the world market has become highly enhanced, most Asian companies and organizations would like to expand their reputations in the global market. Therefore, the understanding of the communications environment and having execution capabilities, not only for the local setting but also for the global market, can be seen as essential competencies in order to manage an organization's reputation in the near future."

Sunmi Kim, Director, Burson-Marsteller, Korea

It is said that when it comes to planning for the future, there are three kinds of people: those who let it happen, those who make it happen, and those who wonder what has happened.

As public relations professionals, we will have to adapt to these new environments and make the necessary changes ourselves on behalf of organizations and expertly communicate with stakeholders. The future of public relations is in our hands.

Endnotes

1. PRSA Report and Recommendations of the Second Task Force on Stature and Role of Public Relations. Public Relations Society of America, (1993).
2. Bernays, E.L., "Bernays' 62 years in Public Relations," *Public Relations Quarterly*, (Fall 1981): 8.

Subject Index

Organization Index